WARTIME

The First World War
in a Canadian Town

WARTIME

The First World War
in a Canadian Town

EDWARD BUTTS

JAMES LORIMER & COMPANY LTD., PUBLISHERS
TORONTO

J971.
343
03
BUT

James Lorimer & Company Ltd., Publishers acknowledges the support of the Ontario Arts Council (OAC), an agency of the Government of Ontario, which in 2015–16 funded 1,676 individual artists and 1,125 organizations in 209 communities across Ontario for a total of $50.5 million. We acknowledge the support of the Canada Council for the Arts, which last year invested $153 million to bring the arts to Canadians throughout the country. This project has been made possible in part by the Government of Canada and with the support of the Ontario Media Development Corporation.

Cover design: Tyler Cleroux
Cover images: Courtesy of Guelph Museums — images not credited elsewhere: front cover (clockwise from top) 1986.18.224, 2012.68.77, M1972.5.5.2.

Library and Archives Canada Cataloguing in Publication

Butts, Edward, 1951-, author
        Wartime : the First World War in a Canadian town
/ Edward Butts.

Includes bibliographical references and index.
Issued in print and electronic formats.
ISBN 978-1-4594-1099-2 (hardcover).--ISBN 978-1-4594-1104-3 (EPUB)

        1. World War, 1914-1918--Social aspects--Ontario--Guelph.
2. Guelph (Ont.)--History--20th century. I. Title.

FC3099.G83B88 2017   971.3'4303   C2017-903834-6
                                                C2017-903835-4

James Lorimer & Company Ltd., Publishers
117 Peter Street, Suite 304
Toronto, ON, Canada
M5V 0M3
www.lorimer.ca

Printed and bound in Canada.

CONTENTS

INTRODUCTION   7

PROLOGUE   9

CHAPTER 1   *July 1914*   13

CHAPTER 2   *A Fight for Civilization*   23

CHAPTER 3   *War News 1915*   37

CHAPTER 4   *September 1915*   55

CHAPTER 5   *The Knock at the Door*   65

CHAPTER 6   *"Will Daddy Come Home Tonight?"*   83

CHAPTER 7   *Battle Royal at the Opera House*   95

CHAPTER 8   *Christian Soldiers*   107

CHAPTER 9   *Conscription: The Novitiate Raid*   117

CHAPTER 10 *Unsung Heroes and Angels of Mercy*   135

CHAPTER 11 *"It's a Happy Trench that has Black Cats in it"*   145

CHAPTER 12 *Any Name But Berlin*   153

CHAPTER 13 *Spartan Mothers and White Feathers*   167

CHAPTER 14 *Socks and Machine Guns*   179

CHAPTER 15 *Spies and Saboteurs*   193

CHAPTER 16 *Shortages and the Battle of Guelph*   205

CHAPTER 17 *Conscription: A Rough Night for Socialists*   217

CHAPTER 18 *War News 1918*   233

CHAPTER 19 *Homecoming*   243

CHAPTER 20 *Aftermath*   259

ACKNOWLEDGEMENTS   274

BIBLIOGRAPHY   275

INDEX   277

For the Peacemakers

INTRODUCTION

The Guelph Cenotaph is an impressive monument, located in a little park next to a busy intersection at the edge of the downtown core. Looking at the lists of names of the city's war dead one day in 2014, the centenary of the beginning of the First World War, I thought that the only name with which most people would be familiar was that of John McCrae, the author of "In Flanders Fields." After speaking to Phil Andrews, the managing editor of the Guelph *Mercury*, I began to research the life stories behind some of the other names under 1914–18. Initially, I intended to write just a few articles. The number had grown to more than fifty by the time the *Mercury* suddenly ceased publication in February 2016. That project led to this book.

My research of names on a metal plaque revealed amazing stories of people who had once lived in Guelph.

They had attended its schools and churches, worked in its factories and walked the same streets people walk today. As their personal stories unfolded, so did the larger story of their community as it endured one of the most cataclysmic periods in Canadian history.

Guelph certainly had unique episodes during the war years, such as the Military Police raid on a Catholic seminary. But for the most part, the experiences, fears and tragedies of the people of Guelph were those of Canadians in communities across the country. This book explores events in a small Canadian city that was in many ways typical of the hometowns of the men and women who served overseas. The setting is Guelph, but the story is Canada's.

PROLOGUE

Although in the summer of 1914 Canada had a regular army of just a few thousand men, the people of communities like Guelph would not have considered themselves entirely unprepared for war. Guelph actually had a substantial military installation, the Armoury. Built in 1908, the Armoury was designed in a late Gothic-Revival style as a fortress-like structure of brick walls with rock-faced stone details and castellated towers. It loomed over the city centre like a medieval guardian. But well before the construction of the Armoury, Guelph had developed a military tradition.

Since the mid-nineteenth century, militarism had been part of the social fabric of colonial Canada. Mother England expected Canadians to take responsibility for their own defence. Every community had its militia unit of civilians who were to take up arms in times of crisis. Militiamen from

Guelph had mobilized along with those from other communities to meet the Fenian threat in 1866. Some had gone to fight in the Boer War of 1899–1902.

The militarization of boys began in school. In fact, Guelph had the first cadet corps in Canada. Called the Highland Cadets, it was organized in 1885 by veteran British soldier Walter Clark, a former gunnery instructor. Clark was also the first in Canada to organize and train a corps for girls, the Daughters of the Regiment.

Cadet programs taught boys that they had a duty as free citizens to fight for their country and their monarch. The purpose was not only to begin the groundwork of training for future soldiers, but also to lay the foundation for the development of proper citizens based on the prevailing ideals: physical prowess, self-reliance, courage, honesty, religious devotion, good sportsmanship, a strong work ethic and loyalty. The cult of manliness that had developed in Victorian England was perceived as the model for the Empire.

The cadets drilled in military-style uniforms. They had regimental bands, and on national holidays they marched in parades and performed in parks. The boys learned to appreciate teamwork through sports like hockey and football. Boxing instilled individual courage and toughened them up. By the time the boys had grown into youths, they were ready to advance to the actual militia.

Throughout the Victorian and Edwardian eras, militia units bearing various names had existed in Guelph and Wellington County. After a period of merger and reorganization, they evolved into the 11th Field Artillery Regiment and the 30th Wellington Rifles. The Guelph artillery men were trained with old British garrison field guns, but nonetheless achieved such a high level of efficiency that in peacetime competitions with other militia units they won numerous prizes, including the Governor General's Cup seven times.

Militiamen took their roles as part-time soldiers seriously. They drilled regularly, were trained in the use of military weaponry, learned to obey orders and wore their uniforms with pride. Membership in the militia carried social prestige, especially if a young man achieved an officer's rank. They were not perceived to be merely "weekend warriors," but the backbone of what Minister of Militia Sir Sam Hughes believed to be Canada's real army. In Guelph, as in other communities with a proud cadet and militia heritage, many of the men who answered the call to arms in 1914 thought they were ready for the battles that lay ahead. Of the more than 5,600 Guelph volunteers (of whom over 3,300 were accepted) who signed attestation papers, many, such as James Doughty, William Leslie and Herbert "Herb" Philp, claimed membership in cadet or militia units.

While some of the former militiamen did in fact become officers in the regiments of the Canadian Expeditionary Force, and even the Royal Flying Corps, the vast majority went to war as privates and non-commissioned officers. In the trenches of the Western Front they would find themselves in a new kind of warfare undreamed of by their cadet and militia instructors. They were not prepared for it. Nor were the families that prayed for their safe return.

At the war's beginning, Guelph Mayor Samuel Carter called it a fight for civilization. Later, as Guelph's MPP, he appealed to young men to enlist. (Courtesy of Guelph Museums 1987.14.4)

CHAPTER 1
JULY 1914

July of 1914 was particularly hot in the small city of Guelph, Ontario, seventy kilometres west of Toronto. Labourers sweltered in the iron foundries and textile mills that were the backbone of the growing industrial sector. Around St. George's Square in the city centre and along the main downtown thoroughfares, Macdonell, Wyndham and Carden streets, large awnings shaded the front windows from sunlight that would otherwise have turned the interiors of shops and offices into ovens. All over town, the men who drove the ice wagons were hard pressed to keep up with demand.

On weekends, many people went to Riverside Park for respite from the heat. Families picnicked under maple trees in glorious full leaf. Young men and their sweethearts canoed on the Speed River while children waded in the cool water. Others went to Exhibition Park, where they watched baseball games and listened to outdoor concerts performed by children's church choirs.

Anybody strolling through a Guelph park on a weekend afternoon that July would have mixed with a varied citizenry that was as close to typical as could be in a country as demographically and culturally diverse as Canada. English was the dominant language, but the ear of a native-born Canadian would have picked up accents from all over the British Isles. There were also voices from Italy and even a few from Eastern Europe.

In the parks, the families from affluent neighbourhoods shared common ground with "foreigners" who lived in the shanties of St. Patrick's Ward, the working-class district in Guelph's east end known simply as "The Ward." From modest but comfortable houses in other parts of town where tree-lined streets had names like Oxford, Glasgow, Suffolk and Dublin, came the families of tradesmen, shopkeepers, clerks and public servants. One might encounter such people as Dr. Richard Ireland, Reverend William Hindson or Mayor Samuel Carter. Looking across a green field or up into the sports stands one might spot housebuilder Norman Brydges, machinist George Curzon, carpenter Horace Fell, blacksmith William Musson, or Robert Howe, a guard at the Ontario Reformatory, a provincial prison.

One would certainly see plenty of high school students, like Thomas Armstrong and Elmer Hockin of the Guelph Collegiate. Most of the students at the Ontario Agricultural College (OAC) would have departed to spend the summer in hometowns across Canada and the United States. But there would still be a few mingling with the locals. For some, like Ernest Jensen of South Africa, a visit home would have involved a long and costly round-trip journey. The stayover in Guelph was a practical and generally attractive alternative. Guelph certainly wasn't a disagreeable place for an extended stay — or to make a new home. The community was in many regards representative of much that was positive about Canada near the end of the Edwardian period, when the promise of the young twentieth century was unfolding as bright and exciting.

Founded by Canada Company superintendent John Galt in 1827, Guelph had been given the family name of George IV, the reigning British monarch; hence the honorific, the Royal City. In the eighty-seven years since, it had grown from an agricultural centre to a thriving manufacturing town. On Sundays the faithful dutifully attended services in Guelph's numerous churches: Anglicans at St. George's, Presbyterians at St. Andrew's, Methodists at the Norfolk Street Church, among the various Protestant denominations. Roman Catholics were a minority, but their place of worship had been given the most prominent location, the top of what came to be known as Catholic Hill, because of Bishop Alexander Macdonell's close friendship with Galt. The Church of Our Lady Immaculate, modelled after the Cathedral of Cologne, rose above the town like a Gothic sentinel.

Guelph's people and commerce were connected to the outside world by rail, telegraph and telephone. Well-travelled dirt roads led to neighbouring communities like Berlin, Fergus and Hespeler. Two competing newspapers, the liberal-leaning *Evening Mercury* (and from here on, unless otherwise specified, all newspaper references are

to the *Mercury*) and the more conservative *Daily Herald*
kept residents informed of local, national and global news.
Carnegie Public Library, stately under its great concrete
dome, was a point of civic pride.

Horse-drawn wagons and buggies jostled with
automobiles and trucks for right-of-way on the streets,
and electric streetcars carried passengers between St.
George's Square and the city limits. Most families bought
their food at neighbourhood grocery stores, but they
went downtown to shop for clothing, shoes and other dry
goods at retailers like Ryan's Department Store and R.S.
Cull & Company.

On a humid Saturday night that July, the streetcars would
pour passengers into the downtown core. Well-heeled
socialites mixed with middle-class tradesmen and clerks,
and labourers from the Ward. They could see a play at the
Guelph Opera House, or go to the Apollo to watch silent
images flicker across a movie screen to the accompaniment
of the theatre's pianist. Courting couples could go to a dance
hall where the strongest beverage served was lemonade.
Men who wanted a night of camaraderie lubricated by beer
and whisky headed for hotels like the Albion. Guelph's small
but efficient police department kept order. Chief Frederick
Randall had been on the job since 1881, and did not tolerate
public disturbances.

The community had certainly experienced troubled
times over the years. Sectarian strife between Catholics and
Orangemen in the 1840s had culminated in a violent death,
and a subsequent public hanging in front of the Wellington
County Gaol and Courthouse. The abuses of unrestricted
capitalism had resulted in the establishment of unions and
sporadic strikes, but Guelph had never been a hotbed of

labour-related violence. Guelphites had been celebrating Labour Day since 1902.

Although unions had won important victories and generally improved the lot of the working class, conditions in many factories were still far from ideal. Industrial injuries and work-related illnesses were common. Factory owners continued to try to cut costs at the expense of workplace safety. Women were paid less than men.

By 1914, most of Guelph's population of about fifteen-thousand was of British Isles stock. Those who weren't descended from the original settlers were more recently arrived first- and second-generation immigrant families who, in a phenomenon that was repeated across Canada, made their community "more British than Britain." Hereward Cockin (1854–1916), a British-born journalist and poet whose ballad "Gentleman Dick O' The Greys" had earned him minor literary fame, gave up a good position with a Toronto magazine to move to Guelph because of its "English aspect." He had first visited the town to play in a cricket tournament.

In schools and at public events, people sang "God Save the King." Portraits of George V had a place of honour in many homes. In some, a visitor might still find pictures of Edward VII and Queen Victoria. Crowds lined downtown streets on Empire Day each May to watch the parade and show their loyalty to the Union Jack. Being a proud Canadian still meant being a faithful subject of the British Crown.

Ethnic minorities endured discrimination in Guelph, as they did across Canada. The Anglo majority regarded "foreigners" with suspicion, and stereotyped them in jokes and through caricatures in newspaper editorial cartoons.

A 1909 newspaper commentary demanded that all Italians be forbidden guns and knives because they were too "hot-blooded" to be allowed weapons.

Non-Anglo labourers were relegated to the lowest-paying jobs. Many of the women who were "in service" in the homes of Guelph's wealthier families were Irish. Guelph's few Chinese immigrants, unwelcome in the factories, opened restaurants and laundries.

However, in spite of the community's grassroots bigotry, Guelph officials often tried to treat all citizens fairly, regardless of race or place of origin. When a group of college students walked out of a Chinese restaurant without paying their bill, a constable made them go back and settle their account. Two white men were fined $5 each for beating up a Chinese man, and had to pay his doctor's bill. Boys who threw stones at Italian groundskeepers at the Homewood Sanitarium were hauled into court and chastised. Racism in Guelph was far from dead, but local authorities were making a genuine attempt to adhere to the ideals of equality under British law.

In the early days of that July, nobody in Guelph would have imagined a catastrophic war was on the horizon. The newspaper announced the death of Salina Beulah South, 85, a granddaughter of War of 1812 heroine Laura Secord. The paper predicted an excellent harvest in Wellington County, and informed readers that Guelph's water shortage problem would soon be relieved by the drilling of a new municipal well. After much debate, City Council had decided to install sewers in the Ward to solve a longstanding sanitation problem. The most disturbing local news concerned a murder trial.

Prominent in the news was the ever-smouldering trouble in Ireland. The paper published a photograph of Austrian Archduke Franz Ferdinand, whose assassination in Sarajevo, Serbia, on June 28, had sabres rattling in Europe. An article on July 18 said that Minister of Militia Colonel Sam Hughes intended to reduce the strength of the Canadian military's Army Service Corps and Engineer Corps, a sure indication that the government did not foresee any Canadian involvement in European troubles.

For a fortnight, life in Guelph went on as usual. Fathers and sons went out after dark to catch dew worms for fishing bait. Buggy drivers and "automobilists" cursed each other. People hopped the electric streetcars to take advantage of the big summer sale at Cole Bros. and Scott, "The People's Store," where ladies' "classy" dresses were going for as low as $3.95. Factories and foundries hummed, and the trains of the Canadian Pacific and Grand Trunk railways rolled through on schedule. Baseball fans cheered the home teams in Exhibition Park.

By July 28, the focus of the news had changed dramatically. "European War Has Placed the Irish Question in the Background" said the local paper. "War Scare and Panicky Feeling Knock Bottom out of Markets" was the headline over a story about financial chaos in Toronto, Montreal, New York, London, Paris and Berlin.

On the twenty-ninth there was news of the mobilization of troops in Germany, Austria, Russia and Belgium. Under the headline, "Czar of Russia and Emperor of Germany Keeping the Wires Hot," the *Mercury* reported that the two leaders communicated personally by telegram, but there seemed to be little hope of stopping Europe's slide into war.

The news became ever more ominous in the last days of July. Austrians rioted over soaring food prices. The czar took personal command of Russia's army of a million men. An Austro-Hungarian army of half a million soldiers was poised to invade Serbia. British Prime Minister Herbert Asquith pleaded for peace, but warned of the "possibility of an unmeasurable international catastrophe." While the local paper reported that London newspapers had "a much more hopeful outlook," and the British people had no enthusiasm for war, the Bank of England raised its interest rate, the London Police Department called on all off-duty Bobbies to report to their stations and ships of the Royal Navy sailed from their ports under great secrecy.

The local paper interviewed Alexander Saison, an immigrant who had once served in the Austrian army. Speaking for the few dozen Austrians and Hungarians living in Guelph, Saison said they didn't like the government in the old country because it taxed poor people to the limit to keep up the officials and the army. "You people in Canada don't know what taxes are," he said. (At that time, the word *Austrian* was a catch-all for immigrants from central and Eastern Europe.)

The first indication that Canada could be drawn into the European conflict came on July 31, when Ottawa ordered the Royal Canadian Regiment of Toronto to hold itself in readiness to go to Quebec. The Canadian Pacific liner *Empress of Asia*, at that moment docked in Hong Kong, was requisitioned on orders from the British Admiralty.

For most Guelphites, as with the majority of Canadians, Europe's troubles were extraneous. But Europe's troubles were also Britain's, and Canadian ties to Mother England were blood-strong and generations deep. British army veterans like William Baxter, Harry Jones and Charles Kerse were probably contemplating hard decisions even before the guns of August swept Guelph from a sultry July into the inferno of war.

Many Canadian boys, like these three from the Ottawa area, enlisted out of patriotism and a hunger for adventure. (Library and Archives Canada PA-122937)

CHAPTER 2
A FIGHT FOR CIVILIZATION

Wilfrid Laurier Callander of Eramosa Road couldn't wait to go to war. The sixth of eight children born to Alexander and Sarah Callander, he was nicknamed "Grit," not only because of his namesake, the former Liberal prime minister, but also because of the determination that drove him in everything he did. Grit was only seventeen when he joined the long line of young men at the new YMCA army recruiting office in Guelph after Britain's declaration of war on Germany on August 4. Standing just five-foot-six, and slender of frame, Grit nonetheless joked with the older and bigger lads that Kaiser Wilhelm would surrender when he heard the Canadians were coming.

But to the freckle-faced, red-haired boy's disappointment — and his mother's relief — the recruiting officer turned Grit down. He was too young, and although his height wasn't a problem, his chest expansion was short of the thirty-four inches required by army regulations. The officer suggested that Grit reapply after his eighteenth birthday on October 19, and, in the meantime, build up his pectoral muscles. Humiliated by the rejection, but bursting with Anglo-Canadian patriotism and loyalty to the king, Grit devoted the following weeks to a strenuous physical regimen that would make him into the kind of man the army wanted. Like most Canadians, Grit Callander didn't realize that his world was about to change profoundly.

The Canadian parliament did not declare war on Germany. Canada was a self-governing dominion of the British Empire, but foreign policy and other top-level matters of international importance were still determined in London. When Britain was at war, Canada was at war. Nonetheless, Ottawa had the right to determine the extent to which Canada would assist the mother country. When Prime Minister Sir Robert Borden pledged half a million troops, most Canadians wholeheartedly approved.

Germany and its allies posed no threat to Canada. But generations of Canadians had lived their lives under the influence of a political and educational regime that held Great Britain as the paragon of Western Christian civilization. Guelph men like John McCrae — doctor, poet and soldier — had fought in the Boer War because they believed Britain was on the side of righteousness. In schools, all children, regardless of ethnic backgrounds, were taught history from a British perspective. King Richard the Lionheart, Francis Drake, General James Wolfe, the Duke of Wellington and General Isaac Brock were all heroes of sterling quality according to the text-books, and no one would dare suggest that any of them had feet of clay. World maps that hung on classroom walls highlighted the possessions of the British Empire upon which the sun never set.

On August 1, in anticipation of British involvement in the conflict, the local paper had published an article titled "How Canadians Would Help the Motherland Now." It assured readers that the Royal Canadian Navy, which then consisted of two obsolete cruisers, was ready for duty. Across the country, preliminary preparations for war were being made "with feverish haste." From twenty thousand to thirty thousand militiamen were being called up to join Canada's regular army of three thousand men, in expectation of transport to England. The most immediate problem facing Colonel Sam Hughes, said the paper, wasn't a shortage of men, but of equipment and trained officers.

On August 4, as Germany defied the British ultimatum to withdraw its army from Belgium, Guelphites learned that the call-out for whole regiments of militia had been altered. Special service contingents would be raised by individual enlistment, with preference given to unmarried men with militia training. Within days, that was expanded to include married men who had their wives' written permission to enlist. Wives were not expected to hold their husbands back. Meanwhile, clothing factories in Ontario and Quebec were already working overtime making standard Canadian khaki uniforms and Stetson hats.

The first hint that the war could actually touch Canadian soil came on August 5, when the local paper announced the discovery of a "Fiendish Plot" to blow up the Welland Canal, thereby disrupting the export of Canadian food to Britain. The brief article provided no details about the alleged plot, except that the information came from "authoritative sources." No arrests had been made, but the report said certain people in the Niagara Peninsula were under suspicion and the most prominent had escaped to the United States. The St. Catharines militia had been called out to guard the canal.

There was in fact a plan to use German army reservists in North America as spies and saboteurs, and the Welland Canal was a target. The discovery of the plot caused a scare that gave credence to the notion that the cunning Huns had been planning mischief for a long time. How else could they already have agents at work in the Canadian heartland? Day by day, Guelph moved toward being a community on a war footing.

"War Conditions Prevail in Royal City for First Time," said the local paper. Colonel A.B. Petrie, commanding officer at the Guelph Armoury, had received instructions from London, headquarters of Ontario's military First Division, which included Wellington County, to post a twenty-four-hour armed guard around the facility. The sentries had orders to "shoot to kill any person who refuses to halt when called upon to do so." Curious crowds lined the Grand Trunk Railway bridge over Huskisson Street, from which they "gazed in wonderment and admiration at the sentries parading with measured tread and loaded rifles on shoulders."

The newspaper speculated that other key locations in the city would be placed under military protection: the waterworks, the water tower, the hydro station and the gas plant. This would discourage "desperate and foolhardy attempts" at sabotage by foreigners in the city. A watch would be maintained over local Germans and Austrians suspected of being sympathetic to the enemy. Chief Randall announced that foreigners who quietly went about their "usual avocations" would not be molested. Those who didn't "mind their own business" — as the report put it — would be arrested. Twelve "Austrian" residents attempted to purchase train tickets to port cities, but were refused. After a report that civil authorities would take steps to discourage "a certain arrogant attitude" in Canada's German communities, the paper announced, "Germans in the Dominion Must Keep Quiet Now."

Chief Randall acted immediately on a federal order that all privately owned wireless (radio) sets were to be confiscated. Civilian wireless operators were amateur enthusiasts who, despite the primitive equipment, could pick up signals from as far as 2,700 miles away. Captain Charles Tuckett, who had a wireless set in the tower of the Homewood Sanitarium, had eavesdropped on messages between ocean liners, and had even known of a sea fight off the coast of Maine while it was still in progress.

The Canadian government was concerned that German agents might use wireless sets for espionage, and that civilians could inadvertently transmit information of use to the enemy. The potential threat was underlined by a report in the Toronto *Globe* that four unidentified foreigners had been discovered prowling around a wireless station in Sault Ste. Marie. They fled when a sentry called on them to halt and fired warning shots.

Tuckett didn't object to Randall's seizure of his wireless set. Nor was there any argument from Puslinch farmer R.F. Hewitt or a Mr. Hutcheon of the Guelph branch of the Bank of Montreal when Randall hauled their equipment off to the police station. It was all for the good of the war effort.

At the Guelph Armoury, 107 army and navy veterans held an enthusiastic meeting "to consider action in view of the war." After an evening of speeches, they unanimously passed a motion to send telegrams to Borden and Hughes offering their services, either collectively or individually. They also decided to hold a meeting every Wednesday night for the duration of the war.

Miss Reekie, nursing matron at Guelph General Hospital, received a notice from the Canadian National Association of Trained Nurses requesting a list of nurses who would be "ready to go" if called upon. The names of volunteers would be forwarded to the headquarters of the Canadian Army Medical Corps in Ottawa. Miss Reekie's nurses each pledged to donate a day's pay to a national fundraiser for a hospital ship.

The newspaper reported that all was in readiness for recruits being sent to a military training camp at a place in Quebec few Guelphites had ever heard of, Valcartier. It would soon be one of the most well-known place names in the country. After three weeks of target practice there, said the paper, the "best men" would sail for England.

While Grit Callander built up his chest muscles, men all across Canada, and boys who wanted to be men, were lining up to volunteer. Recruiting was brisk throughout Ontario, and "red hot" in Winnipeg. In Guelph, which was also the recruiting centre for outlying communities like Rockwood and Aberfoyle, scores of volunteers crowded into the Armoury. Most of them were English, Scottish and Irish immigrants; "Men of brawn and muscle, capable of standing hardship and long marches," said the report. One recruit, a Royal Navy veteran, told a reporter he couldn't keep his family on three days' work a week, and they would be better off if he was at the front, "as his pay would keep them in the necessities of life."

Some of Guelph's British-born men felt duty-bound to return home and join the British army. Among the first to go was William Baxter, a guard at the Reformatory whose colleagues gave him a rousing send-off before he boarded the train for Montreal. Another was Sidney Thomas, who had gained local fame the previous Thanksgiving for winning a five-mile footrace. William Grayson, a printer, was the first member of the local paper's staff to leave for the war.

As patriotic fervour gripped the city, veterans and volunteers staged a march from the Armoury to Exhibition Park, where a concert was held to raise funds for the purchase of "comforts for the Guelph troops in the war." Thousands of citizens lined Wyndham and Woolwich Streets to cheer "the boys who will represent Guelph at the front." In the park, the band played "Rule Britannia," "O Canada," and a selection of "Songs From Old England." Mayor Carter delivered a brief speech in which he impressed upon the crowd the necessity of prayers and sympathy for the men who had joined the colours. "They'll not all come home again," he said. But Carter added that it was a fight for civilization, and Germany was in the wrong.

A bugler played a selection of calls that included "The Cavalrymen's Last Post," "Reveille," and "The Officers' Mess Call." The event concluded with the crowd joining the band for "God Save the King." The concert raised $260.75.

A women's collective representing the Red Cross Society, the Imperial Order of the Daughters of the Empire (IODE), the Women's Christian Temperance Union, the Women's Canadian Club and the city's churches held a meeting at city hall at which they volunteered to "do all in their power to help alleviate the sufferings and wants of the soldiers."

The women canvassed the city, knocking on doors and asking for donations. To their surprise, they collected $131 in the Ward, much of it in nickels and dimes from Italian residents. The Ward was the part of Guelph in which, in the newspaper's words, "hard times have been most severely felt." The contributions of the working poor almost equalled the amounts gathered in some of Guelph's more affluent neighbourhoods.

The total sum of $1,800 was disappointing. The paper recalled that in 1900 a similar campaign had raised $2,700 for soldiers going to the war in South Africa. "The ladies are confident that should it be necessary to appeal again at a later date (which they trust it will not be) the response will again be liberal."

The Ladies of the Red Cross issued an "urgent" request for women to knit Crimean sleeping helmets (a.k.a. *balaclavas*) for local men leaving for Valcartier. Knitting instructions were provided. These hoods were said to be "much prized by soldiers in time of war."

Newspapers carried stories that not only praised the sacrifices made by volunteers, but were also intended to prod those who were slow about making their way to recruiting stations. Grit Callander might have felt his underdeveloped chest problem trivial compared to that of William Jordan of Hamilton, Ontario. Jordan had been rejected at the recruiting office because he had bad teeth. As determined as Grit, he had all his teeth extracted and replaced with a set of dentures so he could go to war.

To illustrate the Canadian fighting spirit, newspapers published eye-catching editorial cartoons that depicted heroic figures in action. One such, titled "Jack Canuck Gets His Gun," shows a muscular Jack emerging from his log cabin. He's wearing a military Stetson hat, and is holding his trusty rifle high. The caption reads, "I Don't Want to Fight, But by Jingo, if I Must . . . "

A fundamental question on the minds of all Canadians that summer was reflected in a headline of August 19: "How Long Will This War Last." The article, which quoted facts presented by British General Sir Alfred Turner, explained that the Boer War had cost Great Britain $1,300,000 a day — "Sundays included." Based on those figures, and factoring in a decade of inflation, General Turner's prediction was that Germany and her allies couldn't possibly keep pace financially with Britain and her allies. The combination of Allied arms and the wealth of the British Empire would defeat the enemy within a matter of months. "Over by Christmas" was the byword in Guelph.

Not everyone agreed. "Next spring," predicted Reverend George A. Little, who admitted that he hadn't taken much interest in the war. "A year," said former fire chief L.S. Finch. Most pessimistic was Edward Webb of the Ontario Agricultural College, who foresaw an Allied victory after a three-year struggle.

Statistics concerning the enormous costs of armies resonated less with Canadians than the spectre of how the war would affect their own pocketbooks. The newspaper reported that, because of an increase on tariffs, prices would go up on alcoholic spirits, tobacco, sugar, chocolate, coffee and tea; and on imported jellies, jams and canned fruits. It also warned readers that flour prices "are liable to take on wings soon." In fact, the cost of that staple of almost every Guelph household had already shot up by 15 per cent, and further increases were expected. Families were "storing up their flour bins before the flour famine sets in."

A strict prohibition was imposed on any trade or financial business with Germany, on pain of imprisonment. Canadian coal could be exported only to the United States, Great Britain and her allies. Canadian horses could be exported only to Great Britain. It would take some time for the actual effects of such restrictions on international commerce to be felt in communities like Guelph. But news of such unprecedented official action drove home the seriousness of the situation, and brought about immediate reactions.

Ads appeared in newspapers urging people to buy Canadian products. The war became a marketing device. "No War Prices" said an ad for the Battle Creek Toasted Corn Flake Company of London, Ontario. "Notwithstanding the enormous advance in the price of corn and all other ingredients going into the manufacture of Kellogg's Toasted Corn Flakes, they will continue to be sold to the consumer at the regular price of 10c per package."

Not to be outdone, the rival Canadian Shredded Wheat Company of Niagara Falls advertised that the "War Lords" could not reach the breakfast tables of its customers because Shredded Wheat was "Beyond the Reach of War." Its price was still five cents a package. Moreover, with the prices of meat and eggs skyrocketing, a shredded wheat biscuit was a meal in itself when served with fruit or creamed vegetables — or so the ad suggested.

A downtown Guelph confectionery and ice-cream parlour called The Kandy Kitchen offered a "Shot & Shell Sundae" and a dessert called "British Dreadnought" (after the Royal Navy battleships) for ten cents a dish. Each serving came with a little souvenir silk flag. An advertisement for a cure-all ointment called Zam-Buk reminded people that "BATTLE is not the only source of wounds and injuries."

A series of ads in the local paper aimed at keeping the spirit of capitalism alive in uncertain times. Under banner headings like "Will Canada Carry Her Burden?" and "War Courage," they called on businessmen to bravely take advantage of the opportunities presented by the difficulties in Europe. Said one ad: "This is the time in Canada when Canadian businessmen should fight — fight to capture new trade and to hold old trade. To stop one's advertising is to withdraw a powerful offensive and defensive force, and to expose one's business without a guard."

As the summer weeks sped by, the manifestations of a war in which no Guelphite had yet fought became more and more infused into daily life. Reverend C.H. Buckland delivered a speech on "A Boy's Job During War Time" to an audience of teenage boys at the YMCA. The Guelph Rifle Association invited boys and men out to its range for free shooting lessons. A crowd showed up at Exhibition Park to observe an inspection of army horses. The newspaper published a glossary of British military terms that defined everything from Company to Squadron, and introduced new concepts like "Flying Corps."

A special meeting was held at Guelph city hall to determine how Wellington County farmers could collectively contribute to the war effort. One suggestion was that they should send a shipment of oats to England. That was countered with the suggestion that a cash donation would be easier to collect than grain. Above all, nobody wanted Wellington to fall behind neighbouring counties in patriotic generosity.

The heroes of that summer were the volunteers. As they signed up, the newspaper published their names. Behind each name there was a story: the young man whose yearning for adventure took him away from his father's business, the son whose enlistment had caused a rift between his parents, the young husband who was leaving behind a pregnant wife, the older brother who had signed up reluctantly because somebody had to watch out for his more impetuous younger brother.

The night before the recruits were to board a train for Valcartier, a rally was held in Exhibition Park, complete with a parade, band music and prayer services. The following morning, August 19, the young men in uniform assembled in the park. With the Guelph lads were volunteers from communities like Harriston, Elora, Fergus, Drayton and Mount Forest. Thousands of cheering people lined the streets as the soldiers marched to the train station, accompanied by members of the Veterans' Association and the Guelph Musical Society Band. The local newspaper reported that the citizens "seemed to realize for the first time that the boys were really going to war."

The train rolled out of Guelph to the tune of "God Save the King" and the tearful farewells of mothers, sisters, wives and sweethearts. In Toronto, the recruits had a two-hour leave before continuing their journey. The proprietors of restaurants and cafes wouldn't let the young heroes spend their money. Food and refreshments were free. This "treating" continued at stops all along the line in Ontario and Quebec. At one rail stop at a town near Trois-Rivières, a French-Canadian store owner wouldn't accept one Ontario youth's money for a packet of cigarettes, but gave him dozens of packets to share with his companions.

The train arrived at Valcartier during a rainstorm. Due to some glitch along the line of command, no officer was present to take the volunteers from Guelph in hand. They relied on the hospitality of the Toronto Corps for their basic needs. The boys were soon known throughout the army camp as "The Guelph Orphans."

On October 27, Grit Callander successfully enlisted in the Canadian army, along with his older brother David. Nine days earlier, William Baxter had been killed in action — one of the fifty thousand British casualties in the Battle of Flanders. Two months passed before news of Baxter's death reached Guelph. The newspaper reported that William Baxter, age twenty-eight, was "the first Guelphite to lay down his life in the trenches."

This Mercury *headline was typical of those on Canadian newspaper front pages following the Second Battle of Ypres, the first major engagement in which the CEF participated. (Guelph Mercury)*

CHAPTER 3
WAR NEWS 1915

In the last week of April and the first week of May 1915, stories appeared about a major battle in Belgium in which troops of the Canadian Expeditionary Force "Saved the Day." Previously, the only news Guelph and the rest of Canada had of the Canadian Expeditionary Force (CEF) were reports about training in the big military encampment on the rain-soaked Salisbury Plain in England. Not until February 1915 did the newspapers speculate that the Canadians *might* be landing in France.

The Canadian press had from the start presented the British Empire as a bastion of advanced Christian civilization, standing with her allies against Teutonic barbarism. The Guelph newspaper carried stirring accounts of British pluck, French courage, Belgian heroism and Russian gallantry. The enemy, in contrast, was a savage brute with no concept of honour, fighting to spread tyranny. Readers were told of atrocities, especially in Belgium, where the German invader — the despicable "Hun" — pillaged and raped at will, and even bayonetted young boys for sport. The plight of "Little Belgium" was an ongoing tragedy that stood as proof of the righteousness of the Allied cause.

Every Allied success was presented in florid prose as a "great victory." Enemy successes were played down or dismissed as temporary setbacks. The local paper, like every other Canadian daily, told readers that Germany couldn't sustain a long war, the German people didn't wholeheartedly support their government's militaristic policies and German women weren't as resourceful at dealing with wartime food rationing as British women. Editorial cartoons depicted the Kaiser as Attila the Hun, and his Prussian generals as thuggish henchmen. Half-truths, outright falsehoods and the suppression of facts were all part of a propaganda campaign designed to bolster domestic support for the war.

On August 22, 1914, the Canadian government had passed the *War Measures Act*. Among its various draconian powers, the *Act* authorized the "censorship and control and suppression of publications, writings, maps, plans, photographs, communications and means of communications" that might threaten "the security, defence, peace and welfare of Canada." However, in the first months of the war, government and military officials made little attempt at enforcement. Even though some obviously pro-German and anti-British publications had been closed down, no central-ized authority had been put in place to monitor the press.

If recruits from Guelph in military camps were reprimanded for rowdy behaviour, the local paper reported it. During the autumn and winter of 1914–15, while praising the eagerness of the Canadians camped at Salisbury Plain to get to the Western Front, it also informed Guelphites of the deplorable conditions in which the soldiers lived. Much of this information came by means of uncensored letters from overseas that families submitted to the newspaper for publication. Grit Callander wrote a cheerful account of his first impressions of England:

> We are in wooden buildings, about thirty in a building, and it is fine. I cannot describe the country as we just got in last night and this is about 8:30 Friday morning. But what I have seen of it is simply grand . . . the country we passed through was grand, beyond all my imagination . . . My, it was swell.

Herb Philp, a journalist from Guelph who was serving in the CEF as a trumpeter, had a somewhat different view:

> If anything, mud, rain and monotony have increased, rather than decreased, in the camp of the Canadians. The War Office has apparently become attached to its own idea of hurling the Canucks against the Germans in its own sweet time. For despite the eagerness of practically every man in the contingent to be 'over the way', we are still wallowing about in England's mud . . . so far as excitement and entertainment are concerned, Salisbury Plains still runs a close second to the grave.

Then the news that Canadians at home wanted to hear

finally hit the papers. The CEF had not only saved the day in a critical battle, but had also achieved the remarkable feat under extraordinary circumstances.

The CEF's first great moment of glory in the war came about more by accident than design.

The British High Command, which considered the Canadians second-rate colonial auxiliaries, had ordered them into the trenches of the Ypres Salient, one of the most dangerous locations on the Western Front. A German attack was not expected, and the Canadians were there to temporarily relieve the battle-hardened British Tommies.

The Allies were taken completely by surprise on April 22, when the Germans opened the valves of 5,500 canisters and sent yellow clouds of deadly chlorine gas rolling toward a section of trenches manned by French colonial troops. As men fell gasping and choking, their comrades fled in terror. They left a gaping breach in the Allied defences. Fearful that the Germans would pour through the gap and outflank the Allied army, the generals sent the nearest troops, the Canadians, to plug the hole and halt the German advance. Against all odds, the Canadians prevented a catastrophe.

The battle that opened with the first-ever use of chlorine gas in wartime lasted a month. Reports that reached Canadian newspapers were often incomplete and distorted. Articles focused on small pieces of what was a panoramic puzzle. Because of a heroic, successful counterattack the Canadians made at a place called Langemarck, newspapers named the overall engagement the Battle of Langemarck. Only later would it officially be called the Second Battle of Ypres.

In fits and starts, news that had already been through British censors crossed the sea via the trans-Atlantic cable, and was then telegraphed to cities across Canada. The headlines were exhilarating. "All Despatches [*sic*] Mention Canadians," "Hell Turned Loose on the Western Front," "They Stood Fast."

But the tales of heroism were tainted by horror. There were stories of German soldiers bayonetting wounded Canadians, and German artillery deliberately targeting medical dressing stations. One Canadian soldier told a war correspondent that his company "had been mown down like sheep."

Then there was that terrible word *gas*! No one in Guelph had ever before heard of such a weapon. The very idea was horrific. It was bad enough thinking that one's son, husband, brother, could be killed by a bullet or an artillery shell. But the thought of a loved one choking his life away in drawn-out agony was the stuff of waking nightmares.

The first casualty list appeared in the Guelph newspaper on April 28. As of noon that day, the newspaper had received the names of 131 officers killed, wounded and missing. The names of privates had not yet come in. Among the wounded officers was Captain Peter Pick of Fergus. He had been a militia officer in Wellington County's 30th Battalion of Rifles for years, and was well known in Guelph.

For months, Canadians had been reading about battles in which men were killed by the thousands, but this was the first time the fallen were their own kin and neighbours. The length of the list was startling, and it was only the beginning. There were no Guelph names on it, but in homes all over the city families hoped and prayed, and braced themselves for what might come.

On May 3, the paper reported that Jane Mitchell of Elizabeth Street had been informed by telegram from the office of the Adjutant General in Ottawa that her son, Private Robert Mitchell, had been wounded. He was the

first Guelph man in the CEF to be named in the local newspaper as a casualty. Two days later it reported that Private
Leonard Peer of Alice Street had been wounded.

County Judge Lewis M. Hayes was the first Guelph resi-
dent to learn that a family member had been killed at the
Western Front. But he didn't get the bad news by telegram.
Moreover, the information was incorrect.

About May 10, the judge read an article in the Toronto
News which said that Stuart Hayes and his friend Keith
Cumberland of Peterborough had died in the Battle of
Langemarck. Because of the mention of Cumberland's
name, Judge Hayes knew that the Stuart Hayes in the story
had to be his son. But he'd received no official notice.

Hayes scanned the casualty lists in the newspapers.
Stuart's name wasn't there. Hoping the newspaper report
was in error, he wired the office of the Adjutant General
in Ottawa. He received a reply stating that Stuart had been
reported missing in action.

That, too, was an error. Stuart Hayes was actually lying
wounded in a hospital. The judge was eventually informed
of that, but his relief that his son was still alive was soon
dashed. Stuart died from his wounds in June. The Hayes
family tragedy was played out in the pages of the local paper.
It wouldn't be the last time the newspapers and the military
bureaucracy combined to bungle a casualty report.

Private Walter F. Angell was the first Guelph man serving with the CEF whose death was accurately reported.
He'd died on May 8. In a May 22 obituary under the
heading "Gave His Life," the newspaper provided a brief
background of the soldier and his family. The format would
become standard. Officers and the sons of Guelph's most
prominent families would be given more column space, but

all fallen Guelph men, including privates from working-class families, would get a front page obituary. The basic information would usually be accompanied by a few lines describing the deceased as a good fellow who was well liked, and an expression of the community's sympathy for his family.

As Guelph's baptism of fear and grief passed day by day, residents learned of more local families stricken by the war. Mr. and Mrs. J.R. Coleman of Crimea Street had seen their son Vincent's name in a Toronto newspaper's list of Canadians being held as prisoners of war. Mr. and Mrs. Alexander McGowan of Cross Street were informed by telegram that their son Matt had been wounded. Mr. and Mrs. John Thomas of Brockville Street received a letter from a British officer informing them that their son Sidney had been killed in action. Sidney, who had earned local fame two years earlier by winning a Thanksgiving Day footrace, had gone to England in 1914 to join the British army.

While casualty lists grew from hundreds to thousands, and more Guelph families received the dreaded telegrams, other events stunned Canadians into realization of the true nature of total war. First came the sinking of the Cunard passenger liner *Lusitania*. Torpedoed by a German submarine off the coast of Ireland on May 7, she went down with a loss of 1,198 lives. Then German Zeppelins began nighttime bombing raids on London, bringing death and terror to the population. Newspapers called such attacks on civilians outright murder.

Canadian newspapers had already condemned the sinking of merchant vessels by German submarines as acts of piracy. News that the destruction of the *Lusitania* was being celebrated in Berlin was further proof, said outraged editorial writers, of the depth of Hun villainy — if indeed further proof was necessary after the horrendous gas attack at Ypres.

Through the newspapers, military and government officials assured the public that the enemy would be paid back in kind. The papers said the Allies already had an effective "gas weapon" ready for use.

Meanwhile, controversial reports appeared in the newspaper concerning Canadian soldiers' complaints about the equipment their government provided. Cheaply manufactured army boots fell apart after just a few days wear in the muddy trenches. A Canadian-made trenching tool issued to the men proved to be useless. Most significant was the matter of the Ross rifle.

General Sir Sam Hughes had insisted on arming the men in the CEF with the Canadian-made Ross, instead of the superior British Lee-Enfield rifle. The Ross rifle performed admirably on the target range, but in battle conditions it seized up, making it no more useful than a club. There was no clampdown on news coverage about the boots, the trenching tool or the Ross rifle, and they became the focus of a major scandal.

Letters the soldiers wrote home were frequently published in newspapers. For that and other reasons they were subject to censorship. Officers read them, looking for anything that might be considered subversive, critical of superior officers, of value to the enemy or detrimental to public morale. Even mention of bad weather might be edited out of a letter, because it could indicate the true state of the trenches. Most of the soldiers' correspondence in the early months of the war read like boys' letters home from Scout camp. But after Ypres they began to take a different tone.

The captains and lieutenants who sat in their dugouts in the trenches reading dozens of letters scrawled in pencil were not well-schooled in the craft of censorship. It was a tedious chore, but every letter had to be "franked" — officially marked so it could be posted free of charge — before it could be sent on. The officers would erase obvious violations, such as mention of specific locations. A soldier could tell his family only that he was "somewhere in France." Some officers were ruthless, and obliterated lengthy passages. Others, more sensitive to the importance of the letters to the morale of both the soldiers and their families, were less severe.

Many soldiers, not wishing to add to their loved ones' worries, made the officers' job easier by writing cheerful, upbeat letters that said nothing of the terrible conditions under which they lived. Often, if a soldier made passing mention of the cold, wet trenches or sleepless nights due to the noise of artillery fire, the officer let it pass. Soldiers also had the option of enclosing letters in special green envelopes. They were called "Honour" envelopes, because the writer was on his honour that his letter concerned only personal matters. It might be a love letter to his wife or sweetheart, or a letter about private family affairs. The soldier's signature on the envelope was equivalent to his oath that the letter contained no military or political information.

Officially, officers could open green envelopes and read the letters, but most green envelopes crossed the sea to Canada unopened. Most enlisted men strongly believed in the prevailing code that one's word was one's honour, but they were even less aware than their officers of what might constitute information of a military or political nature. They often wrote of matters that were forbidden to professional war correspondents.

On May 18, the paper published a letter that Mrs. R. Mudge of Queen Street had received from her son Bert, who had fought at Langemarck. Bert assured his mother that he was "fit as a fiddle" due to his good health and God's mercy. Then he gave a concise but nonetheless vivid account of the battle.

The men of his company had been called from their billets early in the morning. They filled their water bottles, stuffed some food into their haversacks and then rushed to their battle lines. On the way, they met the gasping French troops who were retreating from the gas attack of the "dastardly Germans."

"One cannot blame the French for not being able to face it," Mudge wrote, "for it made our eyes smart when we were half a mile from the trenches almost an hour after it had been used."

Mudge described the bayonet charge that put the Germans to flight, but not before the Canadians suffered many casualties. Then he told of how the Canadians held the line for days under constant shellfire.

"Mother dear, you would not know me now. I haven't washed in five days, and am covered in mud from head to foot, and am writing this in a hole about three feet in diameter and four feet deep, with plenty of straw and a horse blanket to cover me."

On May 28, the paper published a letter written by dispatch rider Billy Ingraham, a former Guelphite whose family had moved to North Sydney, Cape Breton. Ingraham gave an exciting account of his experiences during the battle of Langemarck. He'd been knocked off his motorcycle by the explosion of a "Jack Johnson" and had to carry out his duties on foot, sometimes crawling for hundreds of yards so he wouldn't be picked off by a sniper. British and Canadian troops nicknamed the large, black German artillery shells "Jack Johnsons," after the African-American heavyweight boxing champion.

Ingraham was buried in sandbags and had his nose skinned by a piece of shrapnel when a dugout in which he'd taken cover received a direct hit. That sort of information was in thousands of soldiers' letters. But Ingraham's narrative also — innocently — gave the locations of battalion and brigade headquarters. It told of one Canadian soldier whose desertion in the face of the enemy was covered up by his comrades. They thought the fellow was "a little nutty."

Ingraham administered first aid to wounded men, and helped carry them from the battlefield. "I will never forget the sight I have seen," he wrote, "and I never want to see anything like it again."

The sight of German prisoners of war made an impression on Ingraham. "They were a poor looking bunch of men and seemed pleased to be taken prisoners. The French soldiers jeered them all along the line and in some instances shook their fists in their faces and called them 'swine.' Personally, I cannot bear any animosity toward the individual German, as he thinks he is fighting for his rights, just the same as we know we are fighting for ours."

The Mudge and Ingraham letters bore information that the censors would quite likely have preferred not to appear in a newspaper. Enemy spies were everywhere, and they read the papers — or so it was believed. Moreover, the military didn't want the public reading about soldiers writing from shell holes, desertion and sympathy for enemy prisoners.

On May 26, the paper introduced a feature that would continue for the duration of the war. Initially titled "Letters from the Battle Line," it was a section in which "Guelph Friends Hear From the Boys Who Are Fighting the Battles of the Empire." The first letter was from Captain Peter Pick.

Pick wrote that he had been wounded in the arm in the Battle of Langemarck, but expected to be back at the front soon. His letter gushed with praise for the Canadians. "There were deeds done unnoticed in those days which in any engagement of the S.A. [Boer] war would have brought V.C.'s [Victoria Crosses] . . . among the wounded it was marvellous the spirit of cheerfulness among the men. Even those badly wounded did not take their pain weakly, but like the heroes they were. I cannot give you the particulars that I would like to . . . Will save news until I get home."

Peter Pick never did get home. He was killed in action on June 15. Those who read the letters came to understand a possibility of which every soldier was conscious: that each letter might be his last.

On June 1, the heading for the soldiers' letters section was changed to "From the Firing Line." The page included a letter from Grit Callander, who was still in camp in England. "There is no mistaking that the country is at war," he wrote. "Really, the people of Canada don't know what war is. Every day the train loads of wounded pass through here on their way to London from the front." Callander was nonetheless anxious to get into the fight. "The sooner the better," he wrote.

Among the letters published over the following weeks were several from men who had been wounded and were recovering in hospital. Private Stanley Smith, whose arm had been pierced by a bayonet, wrote, "I want to go back and pay my little debt to the poor Hun who gets in the way of a bullet from my rifle . . . Either I will go down, or the German will. They can't fight square; they have to use gas."

Leonard Peer told his sister he was afraid that his fighting days were over. He had a bullet in his chest that the doctors said couldn't be removed because the surgery would be too dangerous. He was disappointed that he was to be sent home and discharged, but said, "I suppose it can't be helped."

Private Adam "Addie" Heller of Puslinch Township hadn't been wounded, but wrote of a friend named

Charley who "got an eye knocked out and otherwise badly wounded. He was reported killed but later we found he wasn't."

The paper noted that Heller's letter bore a message from Captain Pick; probably the last he ever wrote. It was for Heller's mother:

> I am just censoring your son's letter and you will kindly pardon me if I add a postscript. You have every reason to be proud of your son. I was near him in the action of 2nd April, and he did good work, showed no sign of nervousness, and helped to win the name that the critics seem to think is due Canadians. However, they all did well that day, and since. Pardon my taking this liberty, and give my respects to Mr. Heller.

Captain Pick's note on Heller's letter was the first on record of the many messages to reach Guelph after the writer had died.

The heroics of the CEF at Ypres had indeed saved the day for the Allies. The Canadians, previously underestimated as second-rate soldiers, had proven that they were equal to any troops on the Western Front. Canadian newspapers celebrated their accomplishment. Hometown boys became heroes.

"Covered themselves in glory" was a phrase that first appeared in the papers after Ypres, and would be used frequently. But the accounts of the men who were there were grim testimony that the gold of glory was thin glitter over the ugly truth. A powerful letter from Herb Philp was published in the local paper on June 5. It had been written in Belgium after the Battle of Langemarck:

I don't know why I am writing this at present. We are likely to be blown to shreds if the Bosches [Germans] aren't more careful with those shells of theirs. I don't know what day it is or what the date. I've lost all track of time. All I know is that since the evening when the French came running back like a flock of scared sheep, we have been knuckling down every hour of the day and night, giving Canadian hell for every inch of the cowardly sulphurous Hades the Germans threw at us. Most of our battalions have been relieved; the remnants are receiving a brief respite, but we still have some advanced posts up here and it is in one of these that I am now writing . . . The enemy is shelling us furiously. Just over the road, three whining shrapnel shells have burst on the trench. One man has half his face blown off. Another is stretched out, his head filled with shrapnel slugs. There are others, and the wounded are being brought in on stretchers and on the backs of their comrades. Within one half-hour from the commencement of this present attack the hospital next door to us has been filled with wounded and the dying. Outside, on stretchers, men with their legs and arms shattered and their bodies full of lead are shivering in the chilly air . . . And on that slight rise just ahead of us, a long line of khaki is advancing. Men drop by the score and men are blown to nothing. But the long line still advances, though parts of it are clouded in the thick yellow smoke of the enemy's dastardly gas shells. These shells burst with a loud "bang!" after which you see a red ball of fire. The heavy cloud of fumes which bursts forth from this ball of fire makes you almost helpless with suffocation. Even now streams of wounded are coming in, choking and gasping and spitting. They call for water and sugar. Our enemy must feel good to have found such a cowardly way of fighting . . . The last few days have been crammed full of working and fighting and nightmares and sad but half-pleasant memories that will live in our thoughts until the end of our days. Comrades with whom we have slept and worked and squeezed out of it as best we could, companions whom we have learned to love; they are now in their grave with a plain unboasting cross at their heads, or they have been blown out of existence. Good comrades and hard fighters they were . . .

I would like to tell you all about the three days' fight, but I cannot. Even though I had been through every bit of it, from one end of the line to the other, I could not tell you. It is a thing a man does not like to talk about, unless it be to one of his comrades who has fought through it all.

At the time that Philp's vivid chronicle appeared, no soldier returned from the battlefields had yet set foot in Guelph. Three weeks later, Gunner H. Warren stopped over at the King Edward Hotel on his way from Toronto to London. His name had already appeared in the press because he claimed to be having difficulties with the government concerning his pension. Warren's arrival in town drew a crowd, including a local reporter who got his story.

Warren said he had come to Canada from England as a youth, and joined the North West Mounted Police. He was posted in the Yukon Territory during the Klondike Gold Rush. He enlisted in the army during the Boer War, and was wounded in South Africa. Warren was employed as an investigator with the Canadian Pacific Railway when the Great War broke out. He enlisted in Montreal.

Warren was badly wounded at Ypres. He was already afflicted with scabies when he was taken to hospital. While he was bed-ridden he developed bronchitis.

Warren was invalidated and shipped back to Montreal on the SS *Metagama*. Soldiers on the ship were confined to steerage quarters, and guards were placed at the companionways to prevent them from going to the upper decks. In Montreal, Warren was discharged with $39.50 pay that was owing to him for active service. He was told he wasn't entitled to any "sick pay."

Warren's health had deteriorated to the point where he was not expected to live much longer if he didn't receive adequate medical care. The Canadian Patriotic Fund (CPF) of Montreal paid for treatment in a hospital there, and advised him to apply to the government for help. It was probably the CPF that provided Warren with money to go to Ottawa, where he met Sir Robert Borden. Warren told the reporter the prime minister was "a thorough gentleman, aye, every inch of him." He was also informed that Sir Sam Hughes was personally looking into his case.

Warren was finally told that he was entitled to a settlement of $1,500 for total disablement. However, the bureaucratic process took time. He'd have to wait for it.

In spite of his failing health, Warren began to make his way by whatever means he could toward the military base at London, where he intended to plead the urgency of his situation and hopefully have his payment expedited. He evidently had some assistance from soldiers' charities, but nonetheless spent three hungry days on the streets in Hamilton before the city's chief of police arranged for him to be taken in at the local Salvation Army shelter.

That, Warren said, was the "bitter reward" for many men who had been invalidated home. Warren spoke of the unsanitary conditions in the trenches. He implied that the lists of the dead that appeared in the newspapers, taken by the public as soldiers who had fallen in battle, included those who had died from disease, accidents and suicide.

"Other things I can tell," Warren said. Then, according to the reporter, he smiled and said, "Haven't got my money yet, and the discharge I've got is no good."

The article said that Warren had lost a brother to the war. His wife had died, and his children were in the care of his sister in England. He owned some real estate in Western Canada, which he had willed to his children.

The press coverage of Gunner Warren's story seems to have ended with the newspaper article. He evidently left town to continue his journey to London, and Guelphites never learned of his fate. But his account was one of many that scrutinized the treatment of returned soldiers who'd been wounded or were ill. Together with letters like those of Herb Philp, they gave Canadians a perspective of the war that undermined the euphoria-inducing headlines that hailed Canadian military prowess.

A military parade in St. George's Square circa 1914. The men in civilian clothes could be newly enlisted recruits. (Courtesy of Guelph Museums 1983.24.2)

CHAPTER 4
SEPTEMBER 1915

"I can tell a real man just as soon as I see him," Corporal Joe Fitzgerald told the local paper. "A real man never hesitates. He has his mind made up before he ever reaches the recruiting station, and when he arrives there, he is anxious to get his name down and be done with it."

Described in an article of September 9, 1915, as "lithe of limb, broad of shoulder, strong of heart, and with an Irish smile on his Celtic face," Fitzgerald had sailed with the first regiment of Canadian volunteers. He'd been shot in the side and in the left hand at St. Julien, and invalidated home. Now he was posted in a recruiting station on Wyndham Street, charged with the task of convincing more Guelph men to join the 71st Battalion. The newly opened station, located right in the business district, and bedecked with flags, bunting and posters, could hardly be ignored by passersby, and was less intimidating than the Armoury.

Wearing his battle scars like badges of honour, and carrying as a souvenir one of the bullets a surgeon had dug out of his body, Fitzgerald didn't sit behind a desk and wait for volunteers to come through the door. He went out and confronted men on the street, particularly those he had seen repeatedly walk past his station. "Everything is fish that comes into his net," the paper said.

Fitzgerald noted that some men went out of their way to avoid walking past the recruiting station, so he strode Guelph's downtown core, buttonholing fit young men who weren't in uniform. Unlike the women who handed the white feather of cowardice to men they deemed "slackers," Fitzgerald tried to appeal to their sense of manliness. The paper said Fitzgerald had been studying men since he joined the army, "and what he doesn't know about men is not worth knowing."

Fitzgerald told youths he cornered that there was a khaki uniform waiting for anyone man enough to wear it. He had a ready answer for any excuse an individual might present for not enlisting. Your mother won't let you enlist? Time to cut the apron strings! Your father needs you in the shop? Your country has greater need of you at the front! You're engaged to be married? What will your wife think of a husband who wouldn't do his part? What will your children think of such a father? You're a student and you're afraid of missing examinations and wasting your education? Wouldn't it be a fine state of affairs if everyone thought like that!

"What we want is whole-hearted men who are not afraid to make a sacrifice," Fitzgerald said. "Many have gone, and many will be needed yet, before the Germans are ground into the dust from whence they came."

The Canadian government needed enthusiastic recruiters like Fitzgerald, because after the rush of volunteers in 1914 the rate of enlistment had steadily declined. As early as January 1915, newspapers in communities like Guelph were complaining that enlistment numbers were low. In the spring, the shocking casualty reports that followed the Battle of Ypres had brought home the reality of the Western Front. By September, the war had been raging for over a year, and there was no sign that the Germans were about to be ground into the dust.

Of greatest concern to the Canadian government, the military and the war's most fervent civilian supporters was the fact that 70 per cent of the men already serving in the Canadian Expeditionary Force (CEF) were immigrants from the British Isles. Many of them, like Fitzgerald and fellow Guelph volunteers Archibald Ambrous, Vincent Bowen, James Crane and Charles Kerse, had been in Canada only a few years when the war broke out. Where were all the stout-hearted Canadian-born men? As a local newspaper editor lamented, "the old countrymen are putting their Canadian brothers to shame."

Corporal Fitzgerald's "personal approach" was getting results. In the first week of September he signed up two dozen volunteers. But still, many of them, like Charles Lawrence, James Thomson and William Poulton, were British born.

Fitzgerald had told the paper that women, intentionally or not, "are the cause of some of the boys not taking the shilling." While he was being interviewed, Fitzgerald tried to corner "a likely looking chap" in the recruiting station's doorway. The young man escaped before Fitzgerald could make his pitch.

"There you are now," Fitzgerald said. "I'll bet that fellow has a sweetheart, or mother or sister, who is afraid if he goes over he will be shot up and they will lose him."

That September a series of rallies was held at the Guelph Opera House as part of a national recruiting drive. Between prayers and patriotic songs, prominent speakers addressed the various issues that were thought to be holding native-born Canadians back. Hugh Guthrie, Guelph's federal MP, made a passionate appeal for women to do their part. "The minds and hearts of the women must be in the work," he said. "They must say to their husbands and sons, 'Go!' There must be no holding back. Every man who is capable physically and mentally should go." He added that soldiering was a good job, with good pay.

Former Mayor Sam Carter, now Guelph's MPP, took up the rhetorical baton. "We appeal to the young men, who will be ashamed of themselves someday if they don't go . . . if you go and die — and I expect some to die, your father and mother will have reason to remember you. You shall never regret going."

Canadian newspapers had recently reported the bombing attacks German Zeppelins had made on London, which had resulted in a surge of enlistments at British recruiting stations. Alderman T.J. Hannigan addressed the notion that Canadians were complacent because Germany did not pose any such threat to Canada. He reminded his audience that Canada owed a great deal to Britain.

"If tonight you can lie down in peace and tomorrow go about your daily pursuits, you owe it to the British navy, which has kept the seas clear. If by any chance Britain was defeated in the North Sea, the home guard would never stop the Germans from coming up the St. Lawrence . . . If the

Germans ever conquered Canada, all property would revert to the German crown. Not only people out of work, but the people with a stake in the country have a right to go out and fight for it."

Hannigan also addressed the "problem" of women. He urged mothers and sweethearts to let their sons and lovers go; to *encourage* them to go. Women had always been ready to do their duty, he said, and he was confident that they were ready and willing to do so now in their country's time of need.

Reverend W.D. Spence urged wives, mothers and sweethearts not to hinder the men of Guelph.

Major James Tolmie, an army chaplain and the MPP for North Essex, opened with a lecture on the crosses of St. George, St. Andrew and St. Patrick, which make up the Union Jack. "The cross stands for sacrifice," he said, "and therefore it is up to the young men to enlist."

Tolmie then turned to Germany's hatred of Britain. "Germany would arrange peace terms with Russia and France, and even give little Belgium back to her people, if by so doing she would be left free to reek [*sic*] vengeance on Britain." He, too, warned that if Britain were defeated, "the German flag would wave over Canada."

While the recruiting rallies were being held in the Opera House, a hard-hitting sermon titled "The Call of the War From the Standpoint of the Christian" appeared in the local paper. This appeal, published in newspapers across Canada, was the work of Lieutenant Colonel Reverend Dr. William Thomas Herridge. It was intended to strike deeply and arouse the listeners' (and readers') faith.

Religion was integral to the social fabric of the time, and fundamental to the moral integrity of most of the citizenry.

Almost everyone belonged to a church and attended Sunday services. They went to church-sponsored picnics, bazaars and dances. Most homes had a family Bible, and children were taught its stories and lessons. Priests and ministers were trusted figures of authority. The opinions of a respected cleric like Reverend Herridge carried weight. Herridge opened with a passage from the Gospel of St. Luke. "He that hath no sword, let him sell his garment and buy one."

With those words, Herridge explained, Jesus Christ encouraged Christians to sweep the earth clean of the evils that defile it. "We have many faults to confess before God," he admitted, "But the crime of blood guiltiness does not lie at our door. Britain sought by every possible means to prevent strife, and only drew the sword when she could not do otherwise."

Imperial Germany, Herridge said, had committed acts of brutal outrage and fiendish paganism. Germany would, if it had its way, "dethrone the Kingdom of God among men, and set up in its place the usurpation of foul iniquity."

"It will be our own fault, then, if we do not make this a holy war that fires us with moral enthusiasm as well as undaunted courage . . . a war in defence of justice and freedom; a war which has no meaner purpose than the establishment of Christian principles."

Herridge took aim at Canadian youth who "have not yet seriously considered the question whether they cannot do something . . . to strengthen our national resources in this epoch-making hour." He called for God's blessing on the boys who had already marched off to war, and those who would follow. He prayed for "Divine comfort" to rest upon the homes that some of them would see no more. He called on men to enlist, with the assurance that God was with those who fought for a just cause, as their Christian ancestors had done in centuries past.

While Corporal Fitzgerald urged men to be men, Alderman Hannigan appealed to loyalty to Mother England, and Reverend Herridge preached holy war, the local paper provided a venue for even more voices. That September it published a letter from Grit Callander. Writing from the Kentish Downs in England, where his battalion was training, Grit told of the brigades of "tall, broad-shouldered, deep chested Canadians" enjoying historic sites where brave Britons had fought in the past. "You can see that every man of them is proud that he is a Canadian, and means to make everybody proud of Canada."

Grit touched on the romantic aspect of the great adventure when he said the Canadians were popular with English women. Many of the lads would take home "living souvenirs" after the war, he said. "All the girls for miles around have engagement rings."

A long letter Private John Milne of nearby Eden Mills had written to his parents also appeared in the newspaper. It gave a reassuring impression of military life. "We are all well so far and we like it fine," Milne wrote of himself and his companions in Regiment 2 of the 11th Battalion. "I do not want you to worry about me as I am coming home after the war. Lots of the fellows have been here for months and have not got a scratch yet, but we sure want to give the enemy a hot time." Milne did, however, express misgivings about the new Canadian Ross rifle, which he thought was inferior to the "dandy" British Lee-Enfield.

The paper made sure its readers were aware that 150 men from the Ontario Agricultural College were serving at the front. No doubt that gave Fitzgerald additional ammunition to use against reluctant students. The article quoted an address given to an assembly of freshmen by a Colonel Smith, who was assisting with the institution's Officer Training Corps. He told the students, "If Germany should win this war, you should lose your freedom of speech and thought, and all the liberty you now enjoy under the rule of democracy."

On September 20, the newspaper reported that, for the coming winter, a Canadian Pioneer Regiment would be stationed in Guelph. Mayor H. Mahoney took advantage of the announcement to send a message.

"You young men, perhaps twenty years ago your mother gave you your life . . . It's a great thing to live in such a time in spite of all the horrors of the times. I should hesitate to couple the word cowardice with the name of Canada. But still, there are men who are holding back . . . If this war is not your business, then whose is it? You can't stand behind someone else."

On September 27, the paper published a poem titled "Why? Why? Why?" composed by a writer using the pen name Ark. The poem's literary merit might have been questionable, but the message was clear. The first and last of the five stanzas went:

> There's a call from the trenches of Northern
> France, it dieth not night or day,
> It comes to the men of Canadian blood from
> their kinsmen who're over the way —
> It's a call that is stern as the rugged peak, as
> it pierces the sky so clear —
> "Oh, why are you living in Canada, when we
> need you over here?"

And should the old Jack be downed in the
fight, should the tyrant be victor instead —
And the liberty Britons have fought for and
died, be numbered with things that are dead
—

Oh what would you answer your conscience
— your God — or how would your answer
appear —
"Oh, why were you living in Canada, when
we needed you over here?"

While some Canadian soldiers wrote home about the appalling conditions in the trenches, others preferred to spare their families the grim details. (Canadian Dept. of National Defence / Library and Archives Canada)

CHAPTER 5
THE KNOCK AT THE DOOR

On September 3, 1916, a delivery boy from the Great Northwest Telegraph Company knocked on the door of the Yorkshire Street home of the Robinson family. The telegram he gave Amelia Robinson bore a stark message from the federal government. "Deeply regret to inform you that 125741 Pte. George Robinson, infantry, officially reported killed in action August 22, 1916." Brief, jolting words that told Amelia her husband was dead. Now, in her shock and grief, she would have to find the strength to break the terrible news to their children. It was a hard duty that, by mid-1916, had already touched dozens of Guelph homes.

An efficient system for notifying soldiers' families that their loved ones had become casualties had been evolving since the war's early days, when no one had imagined the conflict would last so long or involve such unprecedented carnage. Not until the spring of 1915 did the First Division of the CEF engage in full-scale conflict, first in a clash at Neuve Chapelle, and then in the Second Battle of Ypres. That was when Guelph families first felt the cold hand of war.

Until then, the war had seemed far away. The front pages were dominated by stories about the *Lusitania*, the British passenger liner that had been sunk by a German submarine on May 7. The newspaper reported that about a hundred Ontario residents had been on the ship, but none were from Guelph.

The paper noted that since the start of the war, there had been an increase in the numbers of newborn babies in Guelph named George and Mary; perhaps a reflection of loyalty to the king and queen. Empire Day was celebrated with rousing speeches given by city fathers, and patriotic songs sung by children. In the midst of events both commonplace and extraordinary, came the first reports that would leave the community staggered.

Mrs. J. Mitchell of Elizabeth Street was informed by telegram that her son Robert had been wounded. "Further particulars when available will be sent to you."

Judge Hayes learned his son Stuart was "missing and presumed dead." "Missing and presumed dead" were haunting words that left families in an emotional purgatory, and Judge Hayes wasn't the only Guelphite to encounter them that spring. Telegrams bearing the same phrase reached the families of William Waters and Charles Kerse. There was no closure, so people clung to hope, however dim. And if the missing soldier never was heard from again, his family's grief was compounded by the knowledge that he lay in a nameless grave, or even had no grave at all.

Initially, the Canadian system of informing families of casualties had been chaotic. But while the Canadian government was still trying to organize lines of communication between the Western Front and soldiers' homes, reports in the local paper suggest that the British system was operating efficiently.

Private William Green of Britain's 1st Sussex Regiment had never been to Canada, but his sister, Elsie Bennett, lived in Guelph. She received a telegram from England on May 18 informing her that her brother had been killed on the Dardanelles Front on May 11. The family of Sidney Thomas was also notified by the British army within days of his death.

As the war progressed and the casualty lists grew longer, the Canadian government learned to keep the processing of information "straight," as a local editor put it. The deputy minister of militia and the chief records officer for the dominion employed six hundred clerks and stenographers. They worked around the clock processing casualty reports that arrived by wire from CEF headquarters in London. Those reports had poured into London from the Western Front and from military hospitals all over France and the UK. Through the hands of the staff in Ottawa passed the names of all the soldiers in the CEF officially reported as having been killed, wounded, taken prisoner, listed as missing or fallen ill.

Those harried public servants had the thankless responsibility of sending the dreaded telegrams. It was a delicate duty that followed a strict protocol. Telegraph companies were instructed not to charge for casualty messages, and they were not to deliver to homes after 9 p.m. The names of soldiers who had become casualties were not to be made available to the press until families had been notified or every source of information regarding the location of next-of-kin had been exhausted. Staff had to respond as efficiently and diplomatically as possible to the flood of inquiries from worried families who hadn't heard from loved ones for many weeks. They often had to provide official death certificates for the families of soldiers listed as missing and presumed dead, to satisfy life insurance companies.

The information that reached Ottawa from overseas was in cipher that had to be decoded. Every decoded message was double-checked for accuracy, but some names simply didn't translate well in cipher; i.e., Macdonald, MacDonald, McDonald. Therefore, every telegram bore the registration number beside the soldier's name. Nonetheless, due to the sheer volume, errors and mix-ups were inevitable.

Frederic Willis, born in Eramosa just outside Guelph, had been orphaned at the age of six and made a ward of the Ontario Children's Aid Society. When he enlisted, he gave the name of a farmer to whom he'd been hired out, in place of next-of-kin. By the time Willis was killed in action, the farmer had died. The telegram eventually found its way to the inspector in charge of the Guelph office of the Children's Aid Society.

In October 1915, the Guelph branch of the Army and Navy Veterans' Association gave the local paper a letter it had received from Corporal Daniel Farnsworth, a local man who was in France with the CEF. In an issue of the paper, which Farnsworth's family sent him regularly by mail, he read that another Guelph man, Bert Williams, had been killed. Williams was sitting right next to Farnsworth. Farnsworth read him his own obituary. Farnsworth wrote to the Veterans' Association, "I would like you to go to the

Mercury office and inform them that Bert Williams is alive and in the best of health . . . He was surprised to hear of someone sending in a false report about his death." The subsequent article about the mistake said nothing of the effect it must have had on his family.

On November 23, 1915, the paper received information that the brother of a Chatham resident, Mrs. Ernteman, had been killed in Belgium. The next day, it published a brief article under the heading "Chatham Man Killed," which named Mrs. Ernteman, but not her brother. On November 25, a friend of the deceased soldier delivered "a rather pathetic letter" to the paper. The letter said that Mrs. Ernteman's brother was Fred Laurie. "I just wish you would let the public know he is not a Chatham man as stated in tonight's paper, but a Guelph boy."

The paper's staff members were personally affected by misinformation in early October 1916, when they received "unofficial news" that Ranald "Big Mac" MacDonald had been killed in action. MacDonald, the paper's agricultural editor, was one of several local journalists who had set aside typewriters to shoulder rifles in the CEF. He was an outgoing, popular man, and the news of his apparent death shocked and saddened his colleagues. For over a week, the paper's editors fruitlessly sought confirmation of the report. Then they were contacted by former city editor A.M. Macalister, who was also serving overseas. He was in a hospital in France, recovering from shell-shock, and had met MacDonald, who'd been wounded in the arm. The paper happily announced, "Big Mac Macdonald Still in the Land of the Living — Wounded."

After the Battle of Vimy Ridge, Canadian newspapers published vivid accounts of the spectacular victory won by brave lads from across the Dominion. But in the days and weeks that followed, the telegrams arrived at homes from Halifax to Victoria. Among Guelph's recipients of sad news was Private Stanley Johnson's young wife Emma, who lived on Ferguson Street with their small child. Johnson was "missing in action and presumed dead." One telegram went to the home of Gertrude Cooper, informing her that George Symonds had been killed in action. Gertrude knew immediately that the dead soldier wasn't George Symonds, but her older brother, Bernard Pantall.

Bernard and Gertrude Pantall had immigrated to Canada from England and settled in London, Ontario. In 1913, nineteen-year-old Bernard enlisted in the Canadian army. He was with Canadian troops stationed in Bermuda when the war broke out. In 1915 he was sent to France, where he was wounded in action.

Pantall was discharged from the army "in consequence of being no longer physically fit for war service." He was shipped back to Canada. Meanwhile, Gertrude had married a man named Louis Cooper and was living in Guelph.

Pantall, whom it seems was a fast healer, didn't agree with the doctors, and wanted to get back into the war. He couldn't re-enlist under his own name, so he borrowed identification from a cousin named George Symonds and signed up under *his* name. He put Gertrude down as next-of-kin. Pantall's deception wasn't found out until a year and a half later, when he was killed, and Gertrude had to tell the authorities the truth. Bernard Pantall, a.k.a. George Symonds, may well be the only Canadian soldier memorialized under two names in a French military cemetery.

One of the most anxiety-ridden ordeals for people at home was the long period in which they heard nothing from a loved one overseas. Most soldiers wrote home frequently to assure their families they were alive and well. Scottish-born Richard Henry Hewitt, who had been raised in Guelph by his uncle, Joseph Hewitt, enlisted in the British army. In his many letters to his uncle, Hewitt liked to quote an old English saying, "Are we downhearted? No." He was killed in action on September 25, 1915.

When weeks passed with no letter arriving in the mail-box, people had to carry on with their daily lives and try not to think of the worst. But family members endured worry-filled days and sleepless nights. Would the next morning bring the long-awaited letter, or the dreaded telegram?

The ordeal was long for Mrs. J.M. Arnold of Park Avenue, sister of James Corbett Walker. On his attestation paper, James named another sister, Annie Corbett Walker, of Oxford Street, as next-of-kin. Sometime after James shipped out to the war, Annie moved back to the family's original home in Glasgow.

In August 1916, Mrs. Arnold received a letter from James. Then in late September she had a report that he had been wounded on September 26. After that, nothing! The weeks during which she had no news stretched into months. Mrs. Arnold finally sent a telegram to Ottawa, inquiring about her brother. A telegram boy delivered a reply on December 8. James had died from his wounds on September 26.

The cold, hard military notifications were carried swiftly from England to North America by trans-Atlantic cable. Soldiers' letters travelled slowly by sea. Some of them became voices from the grave. Those were the letters that had been written shortly before the authors were reported killed or missing, but didn't arrive in the mail until after families had been notified by telegram. Ironically, they often bore statements meant to reassure the folks at home. They would say they were well and in good health, and would tell parents and wives not to fret, because they knew God was watching over them.

Flight Lieutenant Gordon Beattie George Scott was a schoolteacher who became a fighter pilot in the Royal Naval Air Service. On September 4, 1917, a telegram informed his parents, Andrew and Margaret Scott, of Cork Street, that he'd been reported missing in action on September 3. The message had arrived in remarkably short time, but that could have been due to his rank as an officer in the air service. Scott was believed to have been shot down behind enemy lines. His body was never recovered. Scott's last letter, dated September 2, arrived at his parents' home later that month.

Scott said he was writing at 7:30 a.m., having just returned to his aerodrome from a dawn patrol over "Hunland." He remarked on seeing wonderfully rich colouring on clouds in the light of the rising sun, and he described his descent through a cloudbank:

> They were ten thousand feet thick and full of rain and hail. It seemed an age before I got through although I was diving at from ninety to a hundred knots. A cloud is very dark with nothing but mist and nothing can guide you except your instruments. The hail stung somewhat. I came out at three thousand feet, a little back of the Hun trenches, but soon got back to our spot . . . Lately we have not been bothered by Hun bombers very much so have nothing to disturb our peaceful slumbers.

As Andrew and Margaret finished reading their son's letter, they would have felt the pain of knowing that when he slept that night of September 2, it would be his last peaceful slumber.

Captain John Playford Hales, son of a prominent family, was the only fighter pilot from Guelph to achieve "ace" status by being credited with five air victories. Hales wrote long letters home, and in the early days of his wartime career he expressed his enthusiasm for aviation and aerial combat. "It is great fun just so long as you can keep the Huns off your tail," he wrote to his brother Ernest in November 1917. "When you get on the Hun's tail it is just the best game out."

Hales also told Ernest that their mother shouldn't worry about him. "Worry is a useless thing and it makes one think of impossible things . . . the number of pilots who get shot down and killed is very small compared to the number in the game and the flights made."

On August 23, 1918, Hales was killed when his plane was shot down by anti-aircraft fire. More than a month passed before his commanding officer, famed Canadian ace Major Raymond Collishaw, could inform his family that the body had been recovered. In the meantime, Hales's last letter, dated August 15, reached Ernest. The language and tone were dramatically changed.

"Recently it seems that I do nothing but write letters of sympathy. My pals are being killed on all sides, and sometimes a fellow sits down and just wonders how he escapes. Fellows have been killed all around me, and wounds are as common as flies in a jam factory . . . Death out here is entirely different to what it is accepted to be in civil life, and the effect produced on one's senses is wildly different. In civil life it means so much and there is so much reverence, while out here there is reverence and respect but it is all taken as, well, it must be and that's the end of it."

Brief telegram messages said nothing about the circumstances of a soldier's death. Families relied on letters from commanding officers, army chaplains and comrades in the ranks to tell them what had happened. Officers and chaplains had to write so many such letters, that the words became repetitive. However, the following letter, which was received by Mr. and Mrs. Joseph Kelly of Alice Street following the death of their son Vincent, indicates the compassionate manner in which the writers tried to extend condolences and banish the worst images from the minds of the bereaved:

> It is with feelings of sincere regret and deepest sympathy that I send you the particulars of the death of your son Vincent. He was engaged this afternoon about 2 o'clock, with 26 horses and men, bringing ammunition to my guns, when a high explosive shell landed from the enemy's guns, causing the instantaneous death of Vincent. You will be somewhat relieved to know that he was not mutilated in any way, except by the two small pieces of metal which caused his death. He was quite dead when picked up a few seconds after. I had the body removed to a nice quiet spot in the rear of the fighting area and buried in a grave which will be easily located at any time. His comrades laid his remains gracefully away with sorrowing hearts, for we all felt keenly the loss of this bright and excellent boy. Vincent was a good lad, and was at confession and communion every time he

had the opportunity. His identity of religion was easily marked by the scapulars, medal of Blessed Virgin and badge of the sacred heart. I had all his personal effects removed and they will reach you in due time.

Vincent died fighting for his King and country and for the supremacy of honor, and at the same time he did not forget his Maker at any time. You have reason to be proud, having given the sacrifice of this good boy's life in a worthy and honorable cause. All the officers, N.C.O.'s, and men of the 29th Battery extend to you their deepest sympathy in the loss of your son, and mourn the loss of a true and worthy comrade.

Believe me, very sincerely yours,
FRED T. COGHLAN, Major, Officer commanding 29th Battery.

Major Coghlan didn't mention details that would cause additional pain. However, men at the front wrote to other people besides the deceased's next-of-kin, and gave vivid accounts of things they had seen. One such letter, by an indirect route, came into the possession of the family of Norman Brydges, whose family had earlier been notified of his death by telegram.

A month after Brydges's death, a regimental clerk who signed his name only as Chuck wrote a letter to a Guelph resident identified only as Alex. In it, he told of the deaths of several young soldiers, including Brydges and his friend

Fred Jeffery, another Guelph man. Chuck said that he, Brydges and Jeffery had been lifelong friends. He provided Alex with a heartrending picture of Brydges's final hours.

An artillery shell had burst over the heads of Brydges's gun crew, wounding all of them, some seriously. "Brydges seemed to be slightly wounded," Chuck wrote. "In fact, he said himself that it was only a grand Blighty and to fix the other boys first."

"Blighty" was the term for a non-life threatening wound that earned a soldier a trip to a hospital in England. Shrapnel had struck Brydges in the leg and chest. Though he insisted that other men receive medical attention before him, he was more seriously injured than he'd let on. His men didn't realize it until later.

Chuck wrote:

> He started calling strange, and in a few minutes was delirious, seemingly from the shock. From then on, he sank rapidly and although we immediately started to carry him, on stretchers, to a dressing station a mile away across country dotted with shell holes, and constantly swept by shell fire, a trip which taxes the nerves of the best, but in the case of a wounded man, it was hell . . . it was dark and all we could hear from Brydges was the words 'I am Jake, I'm Jake, Oh God, Oh God.' But we could not stop and see how he was doing and were very much surprised, on reaching a Red Cross station to find that he had passed away . . . when one gets to know men like that, it is awful to see them mangled.

"Jake" was a slang term that meant "okay." Chuck had the sad duty of sending home all of Brydges's letters and other personal effects. His letter to Alex was eventually passed on to the Brydges family.

William and Mary Curzon of Lemon Street had two sons, Percy and Bert, fighting in France. Although the brothers served in different units, they were stationed at locations on the front close enough together that they could occasionally visit.

On May 13, 1917, Bert was wounded by shrapnel and died that night. His parents were duly informed by telegram. Late in June, they received a long letter from Percy, dated May 15. It described the rare incident of a soldier dying at the front with a brother by his side:

> Dearest Mother: It is with heavy heart indeed that I write this time. It seems so much has happened in so very short a time, that I can scarce realize fully that Bert has gone. Ere you get this letter you will have received word from Ottawa, telling you that Bert died of wounds: would to God I could get these lines to you just as soon . . . I am assured you will find a measure of comfort and peace of mind in the sure knowledge that it's God's will, and that 'He doeth all things for our ultimate good.' It will perhaps be some comfort to you to know that I was with him at the last, and though the doctor assured me there was no chance, I never gave up hope till he was gone. Everything possible was done for him.

Percy told of the circumstances under which Bert had been wounded, and how his own commanding officer had allowed him to leave his post and go to his brother's side. He said Bert recognized him and spoke to him, saying goodbye before losing consciousness. "He went very quietly; he did not suffer the least." Percy wrote that during the time they shared at the front he had come to know his brother "better . . . than I ever did before."

The long silence concerning the fate of a soldier who had been made a prisoner of war was just as unbearable as it was for those reported missing and presumed dead. Even after Ottawa had been officially informed that a soldier had fallen into enemy hands, and passed the word on to his family, it seemed as though the man had fallen into a dark hole. The "brutality of the Hun" was a constant theme in wartime propaganda, and families anguished over how the Germans treated prisoners.

At the Hague Convention of 1907, Germany had been one of the signatories of an agreement that stated PoWs were to be treated humanely. But no belligerent nation of the Great War had been prepared for the overwhelming number of men who became captives, and the articles concerning the use of PoWs for labour were vague.

Irish-born Bernard William "Barney" Hannan was already a veteran of the British army when he followed his brother Jack to Canada in 1910 and settled in Guelph. He was in the first wave of volunteers who joined the CEF in 1914. During the Second Battle of Ypres, Hannan and about three hundred other men were cut off from the main army and taken prisoner.

Hannan and his comrades eventually wound up in the potash-salt mine at Beienrode, a hell-hole where they were starved, beaten and forced to labour from 6:00 a.m. to 9:30 p.m., seven days a week. Through the Red Cross, the prisoners were allowed limited correspondence with their families. Many months would pass between the letters Jack received from his brother. They spoke poignantly of Barney's longing for home. Late in 1917, he wrote, "Well Jack, Christmas is here once again. This is my third in this country. I'm wondering if it's my last. I sincerely hope so."

In October, 1918, Barney wrote, "I don't think there is any chance of my being with you this Christmas . . . Pretty tough."

Hannan was released on November 30, 1918. He returned to Guelph after spending almost three and a half years as a PoW. In recognition of his ordeal, Hannan received a letter from King George V and $800.

The wives of soldiers who had been reported missing and presumed dead were in the peculiar position of being *semi*-widows. The government advised them not to remarry too hastily, in case the presumption of death proved to be incorrect. Missing men sometimes turned up in hospitals, were found to be prisoners of war or in a few cases were suspected of desertion. For one Guelph woman, her husband's "missing" status was due to bureaucratic confusion and some odd twists of fate.

Helen Pollington's husband George went off to war in April 1916. In August 1917, she was informed by telegram that he was missing and presumed dead. After receiving the devastating news, Helen went to work as a waitress in Guelph's Royal Hotel.

But George Pollington wasn't dead. An explosion had knocked him into a shell hole where stretcher-bearers eventually found him. He was taken to a medical station, but didn't regain consciousness for four days. Meanwhile, he was officially reported missing and presumed dead. That information went to London, then Ottawa and finally Guelph.

While Helen grieved, Pollington was being transferred from one military hospital to another — eleven in all. Two of the hospitals were bombed, resulting in destroyed records and further confusion. Pollington had received numerous shrapnel wounds in his legs and back, and both hands had been badly injured, making them useless for months. He also developed a severe case of a bacterial infection called trench fever. During his long period of illness and recuperation, Pollington was unable to write letters. He was unaware that the army had him officially listed as dead, and the error went undetected in regimental headquarters. It didn't seem to have occurred to George to have someone write a letter to his wife for him while his hands healed.

Sometime in the spring of 1918, Pollington finally regained the use of his hands. He wrote to Helen, telling her that he was being invalided back to Canada. Helen never received the letter.

On June 8, 1918, Pollington arrived in Guelph. He learned that Helen was working at the Royal Hotel, and went there. At first sight of him, Helen thought she was seeing a ghost. Pollington assured her that he was not an apparition, and Helen had, in the words of the newspaper, "a pleasant surprise."

The press informed the public of battles and heroics in places most Canadians had never heard of before the war. Telegrams and the letters that followed them brought the war to the hearts and souls of families. Mothers who had lost older sons would forbid younger sons to enlist when they came of age, resulting in tensions in the home. The attestation papers of numerous Guelph recruits were signed not in Guelph, but at the military bases in Valcartier and London, indicating that some young men felt they had to get out of town if they wanted to enlist.

A slain soldier's personal effects would be returned to his family. In the case of Walter Hayward, who was killed by artillery fire, that was a cardboard container about the size of a shoebox that had his regimental number written on it. Inside, along with some documents and sleeve badges, was a torn leather pouch. The pouch contained shredded bits of photographs of Walter and his army buddies posing with some French farm girls they'd met while on leave. It had been ripped by the very shrapnel that had killed him. For his family, it was mute testimony to the violent nature of his death.

By 1916, the appearance of the telegram messenger boy on the street was a cause of alarm. In neighbourhoods in which everybody knew everybody else and visited regularly, people stopped knocking on the doors of families that had members fighting overseas. They would call out from the front step, rather than unduly alarm the household. Soldiers' families lived in dread of the knock on the door.

Department stores carried lines of children's clothes modelled on Canadian army uniforms, as shown here by John Newstead Jr. of Guelph, in a photo taken circa 1915. (Courtesy of Guelph Museums 1995.11.8)

CHAPTER 6
"WILL DADDY COME HOME TONIGHT?"

Edward "Ted" Tarrington was eight years old when he arrived in Guelph to live with David and Bella McBeth, the couple that would eventually adopt him. Ted's parents, James and Lily Tarrington, had immigrated to Canada from England, and were living in Toronto with their nine children when the war started. James had volunteered for the CEF. He'd been gassed in February 1916, invalidated home and discharged. He'd died the following April from what doctors said was pneumonia.

The Canadian Board of Pension Commissioners refused to pay Lily the pension to which she should have been entitled as a war widow. Their argument was that James had died *after* being discharged, and there was no evidence that his death from pneumonia was the result of war service. In spite of support from the Great War Veterans' Association and the Toronto *Daily Star*, Lily lost her case with the pension board. In order to support her family, she did factory jobs, leaving the younger children in the care of the older ones. But women's wages were so low that she finally had to place some of her children in the care of other families. Lily meant the arrangement to be temporary, but soon after she caught typhoid fever and died at the age of thirty-eight.

The rest of the children were placed in foster homes and eventually adopted. They were with loving families, but scattered to different communities, as far apart as Paisley, Guelph and Woodbridge. They lost all contact with each other. With the exception of Ted, who kept his own surname, the children were all given the names of their respective adopted families. Orphaned and separated because of the war, Ted and his siblings would not be reunited for many years.

While the particular tragedy that befell the Tarrington family wasn't typical, it nonetheless was a stark example of the physical hardships and emotionally traumatic ordeals that shattered the familiar worlds of many children. Boys and girls who had little understanding of the war had to adjust to the fact that fathers, older brothers and sometimes older sisters had gone away, possibly for a long time. Those who were old enough wrote letters to dads and siblings. All sat quietly while mothers read them letters that came from far-away France.

One Guelph soldier who wrote home frequently was Corporal George Ryder, father of four. Born in England in 1880, Ryder had served with the British army in the Boer War before immigrating to Canada with his wife Maggie and settling in Guelph. Against Maggie's objections, with the outbreak of war, Ryder enlisted in the CEF at the age of thirty-six, stating it was his duty. Ryder thought that as an experienced soldier he might be able to set an example for the young lads who were signing up.

One of Ryder's letters to his son, George, Jr., was dated October 2, 1916:

> Now George, I hope you are keeping well and behaving like a good boy and not worrying Mother too much and that Evelyn & Rudolf & Agnes are also keeping well. Ma tells me in her letters that Agnes is all the time singing but on one of those pictures that was taken in the garden I don't think she was singing much but she was trying to bite a piece of your head and Rudolf was looking to see how much she was bitting [sic]. Evelyn was all smiles too but you look good . . . I do like those little pictures and am going to keep them until I come home. I can see part of the garden and it must have been dandy and Ma looks so good just has [sic] she is when working hard. Now George I want you to tell Ma that I have just received those socks and the other things that was inside and I will let Ma know all about them in her next letter but oh don't they feel good to the other kind we get please thank her for me and give her one Big Kiss all for me. Now George I have not got much more to say. I hope to hear from you soon so give my love to all. I will close with Fondest Love your Loving Father.

Ryder's letter also included a postcard for his youngest son, Rudolf. "You'll be a man for Ma won't you. I am going to try to find you something when I get to town."

Ryder never did get to town to buy Rudolf's present. On December 4, Maggie received a telegram informing her that he had been killed.

The grief and loss that so cruelly altered the lives of the Ryder children struck many Guelph households. Mother had to break the news that father wouldn't be coming home, but that he had died bravely. Friends and relatives, and sometimes the family's clergyman, helped through the difficult time when children had to deal with the unacceptable. But no amount of sympathy and support could compensate for the snatching away of someone who had been such an important part of a child's life.

The war affected all children. Older children had to assume more responsibilities at home, especially if their mothers were working in war industries. At school, the war and its causes became part of the curricula. Militaristic classroom readers like *The Children's Story of the War* and *Canada In Flanders* told pupils about the good fight being carried on by courageous Canadian soldiers, but said little about the terrible conditions at the front or the high rate of casualties. Children's fiction with war-related themes included such books as *Me'ow Jones: Belgian Refugee Cat*; *The Belgian Twins*; and *Young Canada Boys with the S.O.S. on the Frontier*.

Some public and Sunday school teachers, full of patriotic zeal, encouraged the children in their classes to help convince their older brothers and other male relatives that it was their duty to enlist. The IODE sponsored essay contests on such topics as "Why the Empire is at

War" and "Canada in the Present War." In some schools, children were required to keep war scrapbooks as an ongoing current events project. They filled the pages with newspaper articles, maps of Europe, photographs of hometown war heroes and pictures of Zeppelins, artillery guns and naval vessels. Toronto educator Edith Groves wrote a series of "playlets" to be performed by children in schools and community halls, often as fundraisers. They combined music, dialogue and military marching to dramatize Canadian heroism and German villainy.

Schoolchildren were also affected by wartime shortages of such classroom necessities as white paper and pencils. Pupils and teachers had to make do with lower-quality paper. Pencil manufacturers fell behind their prewar rate of production, not only because of a shortage of the types of wood used, but also because the dyes used in pencils had been imported from Germany and Austria. Moreover, the brass used to make the band that held a rubber eraser on the end of a pencil was in scarce supply, because of the enormous demands of the munitions industry. The price of pencils skyrocketed. Everyone, including children, learned to use a holder into which the stub of a pencil could be fitted.

Schoolchildren participated in class projects in which they sent letters and gifts to soldiers overseas. The local newspaper published a letter from Captain Bertram Blair of the Royal Army Medical Corps to the Grade 4 pupils of Guelph's Central School, who had sent gifts to wounded Canadian soldiers in a hospital in England:

> We are all impressed with the sweet sacrifices
> of the kiddies and I would like to convey to
> them my best thanks. We feel justly proud of

these little girls and boys who one day will be
proud to know they have cheered the hearts of
the bravest soldiers in the whole world.

A letter that appeared on March 8, 1916, indicates that
children were recruited for the major fundraising drives.
Addressed to Mrs. W.P. Gamble, a local organizer for the
Belgian Relief Fund, it came from the office of the Consul-
General of Belgium in Canada:

Dear Madam, — I am very much obliged
for your letter of the 16th inst., enclosing a
cheque for $167.19 as a further contribution
from the public school children of Guelph
toward the Belgian Relief Fund. I shall have
pleasure in handing this important donation
to the Central Executive Committee
in Montreal. May I ask you to be good
enough to tender to those thoughtful and
generous children the expression of my deep
gratefulness for and sincere appreciation of
this touching token of their sympathy with
my distressed compatriots.

Teenaged boys, many of whom had fathers and older
brothers and friends serving overseas, couldn't wait to enlist.
Some successfully lied about their age, or ran away from
home and signed up in communities where they weren't
known. Some recruiting officers were willing to let a lad join
the army if he was big enough to pass for eighteen.

Children were active in many areas of "war work." Boy
Scouts and Girl Guides went door-to-door collecting

money for the Patriotic Fund. For the "Mile of Coppers" event, kids called on people to toss pennies on a mile-long line that wound its way through downtown streets. Girls rolled bandages for the Medical Corps. Children held neighbourhood garden parties at which they sold snacks and drinks, sang and played musical instruments and organized games. It wasn't uncommon to see an article in the paper announce that such a party had raised $5, which the children dutifully turned in for the war effort. Children towing wagons went through the streets collecting anything, particularly scrap metal, that would help feed the insatiable appetite of the war industry.

In the spring, ads appeared calling on boys aged fifteen to nineteen to be "Soldiers of the Soil" by working for farmers over the summer. They would get room and board, and be paid $12 to $30 a month. Most importantly, they would be helping to produce the food that would help the Allies win the war. "Starvation faces millions of the women and children of our Allies," said one ad. "Think of your grave responsibility and the awful result if you don't rise to the occasion and 'do your bit.'"

Like all communities of that era, Guelph was periodically hit by epidemics, and children were among the most vulnerable. Wartime conditions compounded the problem because so many doctors were serving overseas, and military needs placed a great strain on medical supplies. In the spring of 1916, Guelph was stricken by an outbreak of measles, a disease which at that time could still be fatal to children.

In December 1915 there had been just three cases of measles in Guelph. The number jumped to twelve in January 1916, and 136 in February. In March there were

372 reported cases, and probably others that had not been reported. The local school board held a special meeting to decide whether or not schools should be closed. The newspaper reported that when the matter came to a vote, it was "Worse than a Reciprocity Election." Some members wanted the schools closed immediately, and homes in which people were sick with measles placarded. Two doctors argued that such measures were useless because the symptoms of measles didn't appear until the disease had already taken hold. Children out of school would still spread the disease when they played in the street. And in spite of warnings, people treated the placarding of houses as a joke. There was also the fact that many mothers who, under normal circumstances would be at home, were working in factories during the daytime hours.

After much heated argument, the board decided not to close the schools. Medical health officials, with the assistance of teachers, would be better able to watch over the children in their classrooms. As long as the epidemic lasted, the schools would be thoroughly cleansed and fumigated every Saturday. The paper did not report any deaths from measles among local children that spring.

Of course, children played war games in the school-yards and streets. "Cops and Robbers" became "Tommies and Huns." Children with German-sounding names could become victims of ridicule and bullying. Children of immigrant families who spoke their native languages at home quickly learned to stick to English outside.

Department stores carried lines of children's clothes that were modelled on Canadian army uniforms. Parents dressed little boys in khaki outfits that rivalled the ever-popular sailor suit. Little girls were dressed as nursing sisters.

War-related trading cards became especially popular. Kids pestered the adults in their families for the "cigarette cards" with images and information concerning weapons, battles and military leaders. In schoolyards at recess, children swapped collectible cards featuring games, war facts and images of men who had been awarded the Victoria Cross. Newspaper ads encouraged mothers to buy Perrin's Tipperary Biscuits so their children could collect the company's "patriotic pictures" of British Empire flags and soldiers.

The suffering of children in German-occupied Belgium had been grist for the Allied propaganda mill since the war's beginning. As the months passed, the children of the home front became the focus of sentimentally charged appeals to public sympathies. The image of mother and children longing for a missing father was a powerful theme not only for editorial cartoon artists, but also songwriters. People gathered in family parlours and church halls to sing songs like "I Want To Kiss Daddy Goodnight" and "Will Daddy Come Home Tonight?"

For many children of that era, the war wasn't just a part of childhood, it *was* their childhood. Of course, it was a time when sugar candy was a rare treat, there wasn't always meat to go with the potatoes at suppertime and mother restitched old clothes so they'd fit a little longer. It was also an exciting time of parades and rallies in the park, with soldiers marching, flags waving, guns firing salutes and everyone singing "God Save the King."

On July 5, 1917, the children of Guelph's soldiers were given a parade of their own. Arranged by the ladies of the Patriotic Fund Committee, it was, according to the newspaper report, "The most unique and picturesque sight that has probably ever been witnessed in this city."

A procession of eighty automobiles decorated with the flags of the Allied nations started from St. George's Church and carried five hundred children through Guelph. It went out of town as far as the hamlet of Marden, and then back into the city to Exhibition Park. There, the children were treated to sandwiches, cake, ice cream and lemonade. Crowds along the route cheered the children, and in the park a returned soldier, Sergeant James Clark, called for a hearty "Three cheers and a tiger" for them. The paper remarked on the good fortune that only four cars were temporarily sidelined by flat tires. The children's mothers and guardians said it was "the best afternoon's outing that could be imagined."

But for children, the war period was also when mother could be heard weeping after everyone else had gone to bed; when a family suddenly had to move in with relatives, or take in an aunt and cousins. It was a time when you were told to be proud because a soldier from your own town, like Guelph's Lieutenant Edwin Alfred Trendell, had been awarded a medal for bravery, or you could be taunted at school because you had a father or older brother who wasn't in uniform.

But more than anything else, it was a time of incomprehensible sorrow. For children like Ted Tarrington, grief sprang from the loss of loved ones. Other children had friends who had lost fathers or siblings, and didn't know how to react to their pain — or feared that their own family could be stricken next. Then there were those children whose fathers or brothers came home physically maimed, in broken health or emotionally scarred. Even the veterans who seemed to be of sound body and mind weren't the same dads and big brothers who had gone off to war. Many simply refused to talk about their experiences, no matter how much curious children plied them with questions. It seemed to the children that these men were carrying terrible secrets. When young Gordon Humphries would ask his father, Ernest Humphries, if he had killed any Germans, the only answer he ever got was, "I don't know."

Griffin's Opera House, where soldiers in the audience were called upon to assist city police in a clash with rowdy college students. (Courtesy of Guelph Museums 2009.32.1887)

CHAPTER 7
BATTLE ROYAL AT THE OPERA HOUSE

Professor Charles A. Zavitz was the most unlikely man to become the focus of a divisive war-related issue. A native of Middlesex County, Ontario, Zavitz was a member of the graduating class of the Ontario Agricultural College (OAC) of 1888. He went on to become a popular teacher at the college, and a brilliant agricultural researcher. His pioneering work in the development of cereal grains earned him worldwide recognition. When OAC President Dr. George C. Creelman took a leave of absence to visit Australia and New Zealand, Zavitz was asked to fill in for him as acting president. But it was the summer of 1914, the country was swept up in the early excitement of war and Zavitz was a Quaker.

By 1914, the OAC had gained considerable prestige. It drew students from all over Canada and the United

States, as well as from the United Kingdom and continental Europe. Like other Canadian post-secondary schools, the OAC had a cadet corps that was designed to prepare young men for service in the militia. David McCrae, a prominent Guelph businessman and father of the future author of "In Flanders Fields," had donated equipment for a gymnasium. Sergeant-major Walter Clark of the militia had been appointed drill instructor. The OAC's cadet unit had acquired an eighteenth-century cannon. The antique gun had been fired on campus just once, at one o'clock on an April morning in 1913. A single thunderous blast was all that was required for the college administration to have the gun's barrel packed with concrete.

A month after the war began, Ontario Minister of Agriculture James Duff instructed the OAC to follow the example of other post-secondary educational institutions and form an officer training corps. As a pacifist, Zavitz was opposed to any military instruction or drill on the OAC campus. He had stated his views through the Canadian Peace and Arbitration Society. Zavitz believed that Canada did not have to get involved in a military conflict, but could perform a vital role "by furnishing in the best possible way the necessities of life for the people of Great Britain and other countries." There were alleged rumblings among the student body that Professor Zavitz was unpatriotic.

Realizing that his anti-war convictions made his position untenable, Zavitz submitted his resignation as acting president, and it was accepted by the department heads with respect for his religious convictions. But, in a statement to the press, Minister Duff said there had been a misunderstanding, and refused to accept the resignation. "It is quite true that Prof. C.A. Zavitz, the Acting President, has strong views on the subject, but I do not think these will interfere with the general policy of the college in the matter, and Prof. Zavitz, during the remaining months or six weeks of the absence of the President, will look after the agricultural work of the college, the importance of which cannot be overlooked and will not be slighted."

A Toronto *Globe* editorial stated: "Prof. Zavitz of Guelph Agricultural College is one of Canada's most useful scientists. A difference of opinion between him and the students over military training should not be allowed to prejudice him in the public mind. Prof. Zavitz is too big a man to lose."

Conservatives in Guelph were incensed over Duff's refusal to accept Zavitz's resignation, especially since the professor continued to stand firm on his pacifist views. They had been quick to present their party as the one that best represented loyalty to Britain, as opposed to what they charged was the fence-sitting of Wilfrid Laurier's Liberals, who were influenced by anti-war sentiments in Quebec. The situation at the OAC had potential for political exploitation.

In early November a deputation from the South Wellington Conservative Association (SWCA) that included former MPP H.C. Scholfield, Guelph *Herald* owner Harry Gummer, businessmen J.J. Drew and T.J. Hannigan and a Captain Pritchard went to Toronto to present Duff with a petition demanding that he remove Zavitz as acting president. The *Mercury* reported that the Conservative petition accused Zavitz of being pro-German. The story that the Wellington Tories were "after" the esteemed professor became national news.

In a letter that appeared in the *Mercury* on November 5, the SWCA took the newspaper to task for what they claimed was inaccurate reporting:

> We do not know where you got your information, but the accusation against Professor Zavitz was not that he was pro-German, although it could be argued that his want of sympathy with military organization at the college has a pro-German influence.

The letter went on to state, point by point, resolutions unanimously adopted at a meeting of the SWCA: that Canada and the British Empire were engaged in a war in defence of freedom, justice and peace; that every citizen had a duty to serve during the crisis; that Acting President Charles Zavitz had discouraged and interfered with military organization at the college; and finally, that his resignation be accepted "in the interest of patriotism and the personal duty of those of service age attending the Agricultural College of Guelph as students."

The actions of the SWCA brought influential voices to Zavitz's defence. G.B. Ryan, proprietor of a large downtown department store, told the *Mercury* that he believed himself to be as loyal a subject as any in Guelph, and he had *no* hesitation in expressing his great surprise over what was happening.

"Is the man's life-work to be forgotten?" Ryan asked. "I doubt if there is another man in Ontario, or Canada, who has done so much for the British Empire in the way of increasing the food supply of the country. He has faithfully served the country for years and he did it quietly and without ostentation . . . And now, to think that at this particular juncture, a deputation should go to Toronto to ask for his removal! It makes me boil with indignation."

Businessman John Crowe, a Conservative supporter, also spoke to the paper.

"Of the many able, conscientious and desirable members of the [OAC] staff, Professor Zavitz is easily a leader, his reputation being known from end to end on this continent. Judge my surprise, then, to read of the steps taken by my friends, the committee who are asking for the resignation of this most desirable public benefactor . . . It is not following British fair-play traditions to thoughtlessly join a small mob who are calling for the crucifixion, without trial, of so good a man."

The Zavitz affair was the hottest topic in town. The paper reported that from what it was hearing on the street, more residents sympathized with the professor than condemned him. The majority of the students also seemed to be on his side. Another publication, *The Farmer's Advocate*, said that its readers were "very indignant over the unfair and downright mean attacks." The *Advocate* further stated, "There is no better Field Husbandman in America than Prof. Zavitz, who has done for field crops in Canada more than any other living experimenter. Farmers know his real value if a few of the citizens of Guelph do not."

In an editorial that was constructed to bring the matter to a close while saving face for (almost) everyone involved, the newspaper explained that the Conservative party was not behind the movement to force the removal of Zavitz as acting president. The party's leading members chastised the SWCA deputation as "self-appointed meddlers." The editorial said that Zavitz had discouraged the formation of a military corps because, "in the crowded condition of the curriculum it would not be practical for the students to do it justice, and he preferred to let the proposed organization await the return of the President."

The crisis blew over. Dr. Creelman returned, and in January 1915 the OAC joined other post-secondary educational institutions in training officers and drilling young men for war. Professor Zavitz kept his teaching position at the OAC, turning down offers from other schools that would have given him a higher salary. In 1916, he received an Honorary Doctor of Science degree from the University of Toronto.

But even as Professor Zavitz returned to his lectures and agricultural experiments, the war was having a marked effect on OAC students. Many enlisted out of a sense of duty, believing they could simply postpone their studies until after the war. For others, making the choice between signing up or staying in school was a gut-wrenching dilemma. A student might have legitimate reasons for not enlisting — financial, moral, family-related — but faced the prospect of being labelled a slacker. In an interview with the newspaper, Dr. Creelman told of one youth who was the only son in a family that owned a two-hundred-acre farm. "He knows he cannot go, and he feels pretty badly over it." The OAC *Review* began publishing "Off to the Front," an ongoing list of students who had volunteered.

The war also brought to the OAC campus the "farmerettes," female volunteers who were part of the national effort to engage civilians in war-related work. They wore uniforms and performed such "womanly" agricultural tasks as hoeing, gardening and pruning; and feeding and milking livestock.

But in the almost exclusively male college community, their presence was met with a degree of resentment.

The establishment of a military corps on campus had a sobering effect on student behaviour. Young men knuckled down to their studies, and department heads noted that examination results showed greater progress than they had ever seen before. Disciplinary problems all but vanished. But the pressure of striving for academic excellence in a heady wartime atmosphere could nonetheless reach the breaking point for even the most responsible, well-behaved youths.

On the evening of March 20, 1915, about two hundred students marched from College Hill to the downtown core. In small groups they paid admission to Griffin's Opera House. That night Griffin's star attraction was "The Great Madam Wanda in Her Exhibition of Mentalism." Advertisements said you could ask Wanda anything; even "Does My Wife Love Me?"

There was certainly nothing unusual about a crowd of college students heading downtown on a Saturday night, and Griffin's was a popular destination. OAC students could be boisterous and given to pranks, but they didn't have a reputation for rowdiness. However, as the college boys took their seats among an audience that included dozens of soldiers, each one had in his pocket a paper with words an anonymous lyricist had written specifically for that evening's performance. The first verse went:

> Oh, we're going to the punk* Guelph show,
> To see what famous Madam Wanda's going
> to do.
> Oh, we'll all stick together in all kinds of
> weather,

For we're going to see the damned show
through.
The show is on the bum, the show is on
the bum.
Hi oh for Jericho, the show is on the bum.

The song closed with:

Drink her down, drink her down,
Drink her down, down, down
Smile, damn you, smile.

(*Punk* was a slang term for something trashy or of low quality.)

For a little while the students sat quietly. Then, in the midst of Madam Wanda's demonstration of her "mentalist" powers, one of them laughed out loud. That seemed to be the signal to the others, who, according to the report, "proceeded to show the remainder of the audience how little they respected their comfort or pleasure, by the most contemptible and ungentlemanly acts . . . Needless to say, the attraction of the evening went through her performance the same as usual, despite their many noisy outbursts and ill-mannered protests, and deserves credit for the dignified and ladylike manner in which she carried off her end of the program. This seemed to incense the mob to such an extent that the police had to be called in."

Summoned by manager Walter Kennedy, Constable Bernard McElroy attempted to eject a student who appeared to be a ringleader. About a hundred students jumped from their seats and followed them out to a corridor where Constable Fred Morrison had just arrived. According to a witness, someone shouted, "Mob him!"

The outnumbered policemen called to the soldiers for help, and were immediately obliged. The brawl spilled out into the street, where the embattled constables and soldiers were reinforced by a Regimental Police Sergeant named Woodhouse and a group of soldiers who had been watching a movie at the Apollo Theatre. In a "battle royal" in which, said the newspaper, "Men went down like nine-pins," the police and soldiers forced the college boys to beat a retreat. But the wild night wasn't over.

The students withdrew only a short distance to the Kandy Kitchen. They refreshed themselves and then returned to the street and marched on the Opera House. By this time, more constables had arrived at Griffin's, along with troops from the local barracks. The students, armed with an improvised battering ram, stormed the Opera House doors in a "football rush" and tried to force the doors. They were driven back by police swinging billy clubs left and right, and soldiers who laid about them with swagger sticks, chairs and fists.

Sensing that discretion was the better part of valour, the students retreated to College Hill, singing loudly. On the way, they disabled a few trolley cars by pulling off the poles connecting them to overhead electrical wires. In the course of the melee, the police had managed to detain only two of the troublemakers. The constables took their names — and their copies of the song lyrics — and released them on their promise to present themselves in police court Monday morning.

Aside from lumps, bruises and bloody noses, no one suffered serious injuries. A constable who'd been knocked down lost his cap — which subsequently disappeared — and had a handful of hair yanked from his scalp. One of the soldiers who'd been in the thick of it had a slight head injury. The paper said the rest of them, "a bunch of sturdy chaps," were fine, and eager for more "practice" if the students wanted to provide it.

The greatest injury was to the OAC's reputation. Dr. Creelman knew nothing about the brawl until police informed him on Sunday morning. He expressed his regret, and promised an investigation. An editorial strongly condemned the students' "disgraceful" behaviour. However, one student who had been present claimed that all did not happen quite the way the newspaper had reported.

The anonymous witness admitted that the students had gone to the Opera House with the intention of disrupting Madam Wanda's show, which he said they considered theatre of the lowest order and an insult to public intelligence. In his version of the events, the fighting only started when the police began swinging their batons. He stated that he was an innocent bystander, just curious about what was going on, "when a policeman came out of the theatre entrance, and, without a moment's warning, without the slightest provocation on my part, or without even asking my permission, struck me with all his might on the head with his baton." The witness said he fell to the ground stunned, and then, "as through a glass darkly," saw several soldiers attack the students savagely until an officer ordered them to desist.

The two students the constables had apprehended dutifully reported to police court. They were each fined $10 for disturbing the peace and using abusive language.

Another matter, raised by a witness who spoke to the newspaper, concerned the involvement of the soldiers. The disturbance at the Opera House was a civil issue. There was a question as to whether it was permissible for soldiers to "attack civilians at the demand of a policeman without military authority or the reading of the riot act." The paper had praised the soldiers for going to the constables' assistance, and letters to the editor indicated that the public shared the newspaper's opinion. Enlisted men were held in high regard simply by virtue of being in uniform. But did that automatically make them agents of law and order to be arbitrarily called upon by civil authorities?

Any citizen could legally assist police in an emergency situation. However, communities like Guelph were inundated with military personnel. Soldiers weren't policemen, but their presence in large numbers and their potential use as a strong-arm force raised unprecedented questions about the role of the military in civilian matters, particularly in the extraordinary circumstances that existed in wartime.

Before the war ended, 789 OAC students and staff members would volunteer for service overseas. Some, like John Playford Hales, who achieved ace status as a fighter pilot, were Guelph natives. Others had come to the school from distant homes: such as Ernest Jensen of South Africa, who as a teenager had fought in the Boer War, and Hubert Herder of Newfoundland, who was one of the OAC's star athletes. In 1917, the Ontario provincial government appointed Dr. Creelman commissioner of agriculture to advise on food production. On a trip to England and France in the summer of 1918, he met many of the graduate students from across Canada who were serving in the military or as volunteer aid workers. And as the tides of war continued to roll, Professor Zavitz quietly continued his work in the fields and his classroom, training students to be, not soldiers, but what Creelman would call a "strong, useful and fearless class of men who [would] be able to take their part in the affairs of the farmers."

Army chaplains on both the Western Front and the home front had the unenviable task of helping families bear the burden of loss and grief. (Canadian Dept. of National Defence / Library and Archives Canada)

CHAPTER 8
CHRISTIAN SOLDIERS

A Monday feature under the heading SUNDAY SERVICES gave local readers summaries of the sermons the clergymen of the various denominations had made to their congregations the previous Sabbath. The columns for two Mondays in May 1916 were typical of the war years. The Reverend Herbert Abraham of St. Andrew's Presbyterian Church quoted the Gospel of St. Luke in speaking of God yearning after his lost children. The minister (unnamed in the column) of Chalmers Presbyterian Church spoke on the theme, "How can a God of love permit the present terrible war?" A visiting speaker at Norfolk Street Methodist talked about the future work of the church with immigration to Canada after the war. At Knox Church, which was filled with men in uniform, the Reverend Dr. Alexander MacGillivray recalled how King David had marshalled the forces of Israel. He told the soldiers they had a duty to serve God and humanity.

Reverend Father William Hingston, an army chaplain with the rank of captain, spoke from the pulpit in the Church of Our Lady. He said the real cause of the war was that the people of the world, in their mad race for fame and fortune, had forgotten God and their Christian duties. He told the congregation that people in Canada did not yet realize what the war really was.

"Wait till it comes home to us," he warned. "Wait till the number of widows is counted by the thousands, and the number of orphans by the tens of thousands. Then we will realize what it means to participate in this greatest war."

Hingston reminded his audience that Pope Benedict XV was Italian, and therefore a friend of the Allies.

At Woolwich Street Baptist Church, Pastor William Ernest Hindson delivered a farewell address. He had volunteered to serve in the CEF as a chaplain. Now, with the rank of captain, he was being sent to the military training base at London, Ontario. Hindson wanted his last sermon at the church where he had ministered for three years, to be "a plain Gospel service." He told of how Jesus loves the sinner, and how only through Christ could mankind achieve salvation. Hindson didn't once utter the word *war*. But he was leaving his church and parishioners because he believed he had a duty to serve not only God, but also king and country in the capacity to which he was best suited. Men of the cloth across Canada felt the same call. Over the course of the war, 524 clergymen volunteered for the Canadian Army Chaplain Service. They didn't carry guns, but they were nonetheless perceived as soldiers in a holy war. On the home front, civilian clergymen were essential to the war effort. The standpoint clerics were expected to take on the war was established early by Lieutenant Colonel Reverend Dr. William Thomas Herridge, in his passionate sermon, "The Call of the War from the Standpoint of the Christian."

Guelph's clergymen took up Herridge's clarion call. From their pulpits and at recruiting rallies they denounced Germany as the enemy of Christian civilization. The words of Reverend William D. Spence of the Congregational Church might well have been representative of what devout Guelphites heard on Sunday mornings. Spence warned that if the Germans were victorious in Europe, they would not stop there.

"The Germans would swarm into Canada, the gem of the British Empire, and neither we nor the United States would be able to stop the Huns . . . Our wives and daughters would be the victims of German lust just as the Belgian women were."

Speaking from their pulpits between sermons and readings from scripture, clergymen would bring the attention of the congregation to the men in uniform sitting in the pews with their families or in groups from the local barracks. They would have words of praise and blessings for the brave, dutiful lads. While this swelled some hearts with pride, it also — as intended — made the young men who were *not* in uniform objects of shame.

Churches began compiling "Honour Rolls" in tribute to parishioners who had enlisted. On November 27, 1916, the local paper reported that the Church of St. James the Apostle had held a special ceremony for the unveiling of a "beautifully finished" honour roll. Presiding over the ceremony was a visiting clergyman, the Right Reverend Reeve of Toronto. In his address, Reeve focused on the sacred duty of young men to fight for king and country. He likened the men who were serving to "soldiers of the cross," and scorned slackers who hadn't enlisted as cowards.

Some of the volunteers named on the roll had already died in the war: Lieutenant James Sill McLachlan, Private Horatio Nelson Vipond, Private Allan Charles Lane and Private Howard Washburn. Another was Lieutenant James Edwin Devey Belt, son of the church's former rector.

Ministers who had sons fighting overseas lived with a tragic irony. They urged young men to go to war and consoled grief-stricken parents who had lost sons, while they and their wives carried the burden of their own fears and anxieties. Reverend William Ball, formerly a pastor at Guelph's Knox Church, and his wife Marianne lost two sons. Gordon and Edward Ball were killed within two weeks of each other in 1916. Reverend Frederick Gordon, William Hindson's replacement as pastor at the Woolwich Street Baptist Church, and his wife Sarah had been in Guelph just a few months when their son, Lieutenant Walter Heatherington Gordon, was killed. Through some error in the lines of communication, the Guelph newspaper received the information from the Montreal *Gazette* before any word reached the Gordon family. A local reporter had the sad task of informing the family before the news appeared in the paper.

Reverend Edwin A. Pearson had been pastor of a church in Chatham, Ontario, when the war started and his son Lester B. left his studies at the University of Toronto to enlist as an orderly with the Canadian Army Medical Corps. While Lester was serving in the Eastern Mediterranean theatre in Egypt and Greece, Reverend Pearson was transferred to the Norfolk Street Methodist Church in Guelph. He soon became very popular. His sermons were plain and easily understood, and his enthusiasm for sports was a factor in drawing parishioners to his Sunday services.

In the autumn of 1917, Edwin and his wife Annie learned that Lester had volunteered for the Royal Flying Corps, and had been sent to Reading, England, to train as a fighter pilot. The news must have been dismaying, because at that time German airpower was superior to that of the Allies, and enemy aces like Manfred von Richthofen — the Red Baron — had turned the skies above the Western Front into their killing ground. Allied airmen were being shot down at such a terrifying rate that the RFC's one-year training program had been crammed into six weeks in order to fill the depleted ranks. Pilots were as likely to be killed in training accidents as in combat.

Lester Pearson had a brush with death when his plane's engine stalled during a training flight, and he made a crash landing. He and his instructor suffered only minor injuries; no heartbreaking telegram went to the Pearson home in Guelph. But then one night while London was blacked out during an air raid, a bus struck Lester while he was crossing a street. A medical board declared young Pearson temporarily unfit for duty, and he was sent home to recover. He considered the bus accident an "inglorious incident," but unlike the reverends Ball and Gordon, Edwin Pearson didn't have to mourn the death of a son.

As the list of Guelph's fallen soldiers grew, the community's clergymen were called upon more and more to visit the homes of the bereaved to offer spiritual comfort, and to make even greater efforts to sanctify their sacrifices, which they did through memorial church services.

In some instances, Guelph families didn't receive the terrible news of death from a telegram boy, but from their clergyman. When a recruit filled out his attestation form, he was required to give the name of next-of-kin. Most named their mother, father or wife, but some specified the family's priest or minister. The young man about to lay his life on the line didn't want a loved one to read a cold telegram message bearing the news that he was dead. Far better to have it gently broken by a man of God who would offer prayer and comfort. Such appears to have been the case with Thomas Stirling Howden.

The Howden family had arrived in Guelph from Scotland about 1913. In the short time that he resided in the city, employed at Crowe's Iron Works, Thomas became engaged to a Miss Ambrose. In January 1915, he volunteered for the CEF and was soon sent to England. Because Howden had previous military experience in the British army, he was made a sergeant and an instructor for the green troops arriving from Canada.

Miss Ambrose also went to England, most likely because she wanted to be near her betrothed. Other Canadian women made the journey for that very reason, and there is documented evidence that Miss Ambrose and Howden saw each other in England.

But Howden hadn't enlisted to be an instructor. His request to be sent to the front was granted, though it meant that he had to give up his sergeant stripes and enter the trenches as a private. In a letter dated September 11, 1917, Howden told his mother he was in good health. He also made the ominous statement that he had made his will and left all his worldly possessions to her. After that letter, the Howden family heard nothing from or about Thomas for almost two months. They did receive a letter from a concerned Miss Ambrose, who also hadn't heard anything. She wanted to know if there was any news of Thomas in Guelph.

On November 16, Reverend Alexander MacGillivray, the Howden family's minister, received a telegram. He went to the Howden home with the sad news that Thomas had been killed in action on September 15. He had no explanation for the long delay, nor why the notification had been sent to him instead of the family. It might simply have been the soldier's wish.

Families that had received the dreaded telegrams were often left in soul-torturing ignorance of just what had happened. Had death been mercifully quick, or had it been drawn-out and painful? For parents and siblings, not knowing was a nightmare full of the worst the imagination could envision.

Commanding officers wrote letters of condolence to the families of fallen soldiers. With so many such letters to write, for all their good intentions, officers could fall into a standard format that praised the deceased as a good soldier, well-liked by his mates, who had died bravely in the service of king and country.

But not all victims of battle died in the trenches or on the deadly ground of no man's land. There was a depressingly steady stream of gunshot, shrapnel-mangled, gas-poisoned wounded to the army hospitals. From the hospitals came letters written by chaplains that gave families in faraway Canada a picture of dying men's final hours, and a degree of closure.

Major Maurice Wideman, a Guelph native, veteran of the Boer War and father of six children, had twice been reported wounded in action before his wife Annie was informed by telegram that he had died in hospital on May 9, 1917. She later received a letter from Reverend Alfred Bingham, the hospital's chaplain. Bingham said he'd spent a lot of time talking and praying with Wideman. The major had several serious wounds, but was confident he would recover. He never complained, and he often spoke of his children and how much he enjoyed reading his wife's letters.

Then a wound in Wideman's left leg became infected. Bingman explained that in an attempt to stop the poison of infection from spreading, the doctors had to amputate. He told Annie he visited Wideman a few hours after the operation and spoke to him.

"He said, 'I'm doing fine, really fine, but I am sleepy.' I spoke a few words to him of the comfort which God giveth, and said, 'I'll see you in the morning. Good bye.' He replied, 'Yes, come. Good bye.' Half an hour afterwards, whilst sleeping, he passed away. A little time before, he had said to one of the sisters, 'There are six pairs of little grey eyes waiting for me.'"

Private Harry Jones's wife received a letter that was shorter but no less moving, from Father George Sherring, Senior Chaplain of the Second Canadian Division. Jones had been wounded in action in early May 1916. Father Sherring wrote:

> It is with the deepest regret and heartfelt sympathy that I have to report to you the death of your husband . . . He was brought over to our dressing station on May 5th, wounded, and the doctors did all they possibly could for him, but he passed quietly and peacefully away early in the morning.
>
> I was present, and had an opportunity of a little prayer with him . . . I buried him in our military cemetery when some of his comrades were present . . . A cross will be erected, bearing name, date and battalion. Please accept my most sincere sympathy in your bereavement, and commending you to the great mercy of the Almighty God.

While letters of condolence from chaplains thousands of miles away were reaching grief-stricken homes in Guelph, Reverend William Hindson was eagerly looking forward to an overseas posting. He took an officer's course in London, and passed every exam except one, the physical! Doctors determined that Hindson was physically unfit for the rigours of chaplain service on the Western Front.

Devastated by this rejection, Hindson turned his patriotic zeal to recruiting. His dedication and effectiveness as a recruiter and organizer earned him appointments as the Chief Recruiting Officer for the Number 1 Military District of Canada, and the Chief Public Representative of the Registrar's Office, both headquartered in London. His official territory included Guelph.

Denied the opportunity to go to war, Hindson drove himself hard on the home front. He made himself invaluable to the government's recruiting drives by working ceaselessly to bring battalions in counties under his office up to strength. He covered miles, speaking at rallies and from pulpits. As a clergyman, he did the rounds of hospitals, visiting sick and wounded soldiers. He paid his respects to the homes of soldiers who had died. The brutal schedule Hindson set for himself took a toll.

The doctors in London had been correct in their assessment of Hindson's physical condition. He would not have been up to the stress and hardships of overseas duty. Ironically, it was Hindson's subsequent workload in Canada that proved fatal. He wore himself to exhaustion. Then he suddenly fell ill with typhoid fever, and was too weak to fight it. After lingering for weeks, Hindson died at age thirty-eight, on September 18, 1918. He was buried in London with military honours in a service attended by many friends from Guelph and covered by the local paper. The reverend was eulogized as a man whose strength and tenderness were needed in troubled times. More than two years after the Chalmers Church minister had posed the question, people in Guelph and across Canada still wondered how a God of love could permit such a terrible war.

The St. Stanislaus Jesuit Novitiate, scene of a raid by military police searching for "conscription evaders." (Wellington County Museum and Archives ph 20275)

CHAPTER 9
CONSCRIPTION: THE NOVITIATE RAID

In the early days of June 1918, no one in Guelph would have thought that before the month was out the city would be the focus of an explosive controversy that would hit the front pages of newspapers from Halifax to Victoria. The smouldering issue was conscription. The spark was a stunning incident that occurred at a Roman Catholic seminary.

In 1917, as the casualty lists grew horrifically and there appeared to be no end in sight to the slaughter on the Western Front, the numbers of men volunteering for the CEF dropped. Recruiting campaigns to shame unenlisted young men into uniform by branding them as "slackers" weren't having the desired results. Youths like Guelph's Anthony Christie and Arthur Meers, who had just turned eighteen, were still signing up, but not enough of them to fill the places of the fallen. Prime Minister Robert Borden's government passed the *Military Service Act*, which became law on January 1, 1918.

The *"Conscription Act"* was polarizing. It caused riots in Quebec, where Canada's involvement in the war was unpopular. The legislation initially allowed exemptions for certain people, such as the sons of farm families, whose labour was deemed essential to the war effort. However, by April 1918, most of those exemptions had been removed. Strong farm boys made good soldiers, and there were plenty of other people, including their sisters, who could plant, hoe and harvest.

An exemption pertaining to clergy stirred old Catholic-Protestant animosities. The *Conscription Act* initially exempted all priests and ministers, as well as divinity students. However, several MPs who belonged to the virulently anti-Catholic Orange Order mistakenly believed that protests in Montreal had been led by Catholic seminarians. They wanted to use the legislation to punish the students, and persuaded Borden to drop the exclusion clause for divinity students altogether. Justice Minister Charles Doherty, a Catholic from Montreal, wanted to retain the clause for the protection of both Protestant and Catholic divinity students.

The bill that was finally passed into law after much heated debate made all divinity students subject to conscription until the time they actually became clergymen. The Orangemen had apparently had their way, but at the cost of protection for Protestant students. However, the Catholic and Protestant seminaries differed on a point that would soon become contentious.

Despite the general furor, conscription wasn't a hotly contested issue in Guelph. The majority of residents supported it, or at least thought better than to openly oppose it. Guelph's MP, Hugh Guthrie, had deserted Wilfrid Laurier's Liberal Party because of the conscription issue and joined Borden's Union Government coalition. He was rewarded with the cabinet portfolio of Solicitor General. In the federal election of December 1917, Guthrie won a landslide victory over Independent Social Democrat Lorne Cunningham.

Guelph's Protestant clergy, represented by the local ministerial association, supported conscription. The association's president, Reverend W.D. Spence of the Congregational Church, said he favoured Borden's policies because they would win the war. "I must simply stand by the men who are pledged to stand by the boys who have gone from my own congregation."

The pastor of St. Paul's Presbyterian Church, Reverend Kennedy H. Palmer, was even more rhetorical. "From my pulpit I, like many others, pleaded with our boys to answer the call of the heroic and preserve unstained on Europe's bloody battlefields the honour of our land. There our word was given that we would not fail at any cost to stand behind them in the fight; that no petty politics should turn us aside from giving them every support."

Reverend Edwin A. Pearson, from Norfolk Street Methodist Church, said he supported Borden and the Union government because his three sons were fighting overseas. Some clergymen, like Reverend I.M. Moyer, pastor of Paisley Memorial Church, lashed out at Quebec's refusal to support conscription. "I am opposed to Quebec, with her ideals and her indifference, having a controlling voice in the policies and destiny of Canada in this crisis time in our history."

On June 13, the people of Guelph were honoured with a memorable diversion from the shadow of war. The whole town turned out to greet the Governor General of Canada, C.W. Cavendish, the Duke of Devonshire, who was touring the country with his family to bolster recruiting. Over two busy days, the Governor General presided over a reception and civic dinner, visited St. Joseph's Hospital, inspected the quarters of the Great War Veterans, had tea with the local chapter of the IODE, and shook hands with leading citizens. He thanked Guelph on behalf of King George for its hospitality, and praised the city's volunteers:

> I congratulate you on the gallantry shown by the soldiers from your city. They fought and are fighting to preserve our Empire, and hand down a glorious heritage to future generations.

Then the Governor General and his entourage boarded their train for the trip to the next city, where all the formalities would be repeated. The Guelph newspaper reported that the visit had been a success. The Royal City had demonstrated its loyalty to King and Empire. The Governor General had paid homage to Guelph's fighting men. Coincidentally, the paper had reported the loss of two more of them shortly before the Governor General's arrival: Captain Benjamin B. McConkey, a recipient of the Military Cross; and fighter pilot Lieutenant Gordon B. Scott. Their heroic sacrifices would have been fresh in mind even as the Governor General spoke. At that moment, most of the people of Guelph would have taken a particularly dim view of anyone suspected of conscription evasion.

Guelphites did not know that, for a week, while they celebrated the Governor General's visit and mourned the city's most recent losses, the federal government had suppressed news of a secret raid in their own backyard. They wouldn't learn of it until the Toronto *Star* broke the story on June 19. Overnight, the first details of the extraordinary incident were telegraphed across the country, so the hometown paper made its initial report only on June 20, along with dozens of other newspapers. On the night of June 7, military police had raided a Roman Catholic seminary on the outskirts of Guelph. It was actually the climax of a misunderstanding that had gone unresolved for months.

In November 1917, Henry Westoby, a Guelph alderman who was secretary for the local enlistment league, requested that all members of Guelph's religious communities report for medical examinations. That included the young men enrolled at the St. Stanislaus Novitiate, which had been founded in 1913 by the Roman Catholic Society of Jesus, commonly known as Jesuits, on a site about three miles north of Guelph. The novitiate's solicitor, Patrick Kerwin, was also partner in a law firm with Hugh Guthrie. On Kerwin's behalf, Guthrie contacted Justice Minister Doherty for a ruling on Westoby's request.

Doherty replied that members of recognized religious orders were excluded from the *Military Service Act*. He asked that his response be passed on to the appropriate military authorities. Westoby was informed, but he either didn't understand Doherty's statement, or he refused to accept it. He insisted that the Jesuit students report for physicals.

Religious strife wasn't new to Guelph. The community's pioneer period had been marked by hostility between Catholics and Orangemen. Guelph's first public execution occurred in 1847 after a Protestant judge sentenced a Catholic farmer to hang for killing an Orangeman in a drunken brawl. The execution was followed by a long period of seething resentment among Guelph's Catholic minority.

Since the war's beginning, even though Guelph's Catholic boys had lined up with Protestant boys in front of the Armoury to enlist, lingering prejudices bolstered by Quebec's anti-war sentiments led to doubts about the loyalty and patriotism of Catholics in general. Nationally, Canadian newspapers stirred up ill will through anti-Catholic editorials and ads paid for by businessmen who supported the Borden administration's policies. There were accusations that Catholic priests weren't as zealous as Protestant ministers in aiding recruiting drives, and that Pope Benedict XV, who had officially taken a neutral stand, was in fact on Germany's side.

The definition of "clergy" was a major trouble point. Protestant churches didn't officially recognize their seminarians as clergy until they had completed their training and graduated. The Church regarded Catholics studying for the priesthood as clergy from the moment they entered a college like St. Stanislaus. By the churches' own classifications, Protestant seminarians were eligible for conscription, but Catholic novices weren't.

All this fed old suspicions in Guelph. Rumours spread that the Novitiate was harbouring slackers; not only Catholics, but also conscientious objectors from nearby Waterloo County's German-speaking Mennonite community. It was even whispered that, in keeping with the Catholic Church's plot to undermine the Allied war effort, the Jesuits had constructed tunnels from the Novitiate to locations within Guelph, and had smuggled cannons and ammunition into the school.

The *Conscription Act* was initially enforced by two separate federal branches: the Department of Justice through the Dominion Police, and the Department of Militia and Defence through its own military police. The joint jurisdiction caused so much confusion that in May 1918 reorganization placed enforcement exclusively in the hands of Militia and Defence. This was seen as a snub of the Department of Justice, and of Doherty in particular, creating an atmosphere of conflict between the two departments. The fact that Doherty's son Marcus had begun studies at St. Stanislaus the previous February made the situation all the more uncomfortable for the Justice Minister. A series of nagging messages was about to make matters worse.

In support of Westoby, the ministerial association wrote to district military headquarters in London, complaining about the failure of the Novitiate to make its students report for conscription. The association accused Father Henri Bourque, the rector at St. Stanislaus, of refusing to provide Westoby with a list of his students. Bourque had said he was under no legal obligation to do so. Reverend Spence told the press that Father Bourque had "balked" Westoby in his efforts to carry out his lawful duty.

Captain Leslie Burrows of the Provost Marshall's office in Ottawa visited Guelph. He heard rumours that three conscription evaders were hiding out at the Novitiate. (Only one of the three men named, student George Nunan, was actually there.) Burrows spoke to Guthrie, who in turn contacted General Sidney C. Mewburn, recently appointed Minister of Militia and Defence, enquiring about the status of the three men. On May 30, Major J. Hirsch in London received a telegram from the Provost Marshall's office asking why students at the Guelph Novitiate and St. Jerome's College in Kitchener had not been called up.

General Mewburn became impatient with the whole affair. Instead of writing detailed instructions, he sent a hasty message to London, ordering the officers in charge there to "clear up" the problem in Guelph. Somewhere along the lines of communication, Mewburn's message was garbled or misunderstood, and "clear up" became "clean out." On June 5, orders went to Captain A.C. Macaulay in London to take a squad of military police to Guelph and flush out the conscription evaders. Macaulay had instructions to carry out the operation quietly, not notify the press and to proceed with tact and discretion. He was warned to take precautions against possible escape attempts. An unsubstantiated rumour had led to the kind of covert military police operation that most Canadians associated with military dictatorships.

Captain Macaulay and nine military policemen arrived in Guelph on June 7, dressed in civilian clothes. They strolled around the downtown area in small groups, trying to be inconspicuous. In the evening, they took a streetcar to a stop near the city's northern limits, and from there proceeded on foot along the road to the Novitiate. Accompanying them as an observer was a Dominion Police inspector named Menard, who also was not in uniform.

The squad reached the foot of the Novitiate laneway sometime after nine o'clock. Macaulay posted one man to guard the gate, and sent a few others to search the grounds and take up positions around the property to prevent escape. At 9:30 he rang the doorbell.

Inside, the students and faculty had just celebrated the Feast of the Sacred Heart, and had gone to bed. It was unusual for visitors to come unannounced at that hour, but somebody, possibly Marcus Doherty, hurried to answer the door. Macaulay and Menard were admitted. Macaulay immediately demanded to see Father Bourque. The priest was called from his room.

Ignoring his instructions to be tactful, Macaulay acted in a brusque and surly manner from the beginning. He told Bourque he had five minutes to assemble all of the students right there before him, or he would have the building searched. Bourque asked the two men to show him identification and written authority justifying Macaulay's demand.

Macaulay pulled out a document and read aloud a passage that stated an officer had to have written authority to do the very thing he was doing. Then he refused to produce any such written authority. Bourque excused himself for a few minutes, and returned with a man he thought would be better able to deal with the intruders.

Father William Hingston, who happened to be visiting the Novitiate, was a former rector of St. Stanislaus, and was now a captain in the Canadian army. He had just returned from France, where he'd been serving as a chaplain. Macaulay and Menard were startled by the sudden appearance of Hingston in his officer's uniform.

While Hingston engaged Macaulay in an argument that became quite heated, Bourque went to his office to telephone for information and legal advice. Judge Lewis M. Hayes advised him to cooperate with the military police, even though the investigation seemed fraught with irregularities. Bourque then made calls to Patrick Kerwin, Father Nicholas Quirk at the Church of Our Lady Immaculate and Justice of the Peace Thomas Bedford, whose home was near the Novitiate. All three were soon on their way to St. Stanislaus.

Meanwhile, Bourque roused everyone from their beds and told them to get dressed and assemble in the refectory. The bewildered group included nineteen senior and eight junior students, eleven lay brothers and six faculty. Also present was another visitor: Reverend William Power, the head of the Jesuit Order in Canada. A man whose forceful personality had earned him the nickname "Will-Power," he was not at all intimidated by the military police.

Macaulay didn't find any secret tunnels, hidden weapons or hiding Mennonites. But he was certain the Novitiate was a nest of conscription evaders. He decided to interview everybody, one by one, in the presence of the assembled group. His first subject was Brother Leo FitzGerald, who wasn't even Canadian, but an American from Rhode Island.

Marcus Doherty later recalled, "Being a nervous, high-strung fellow, he [FitzGerald] was at first rather indefinite in his answers. Finally he blurted out, "I am an American citizen."

Evidently believing that FitzGerald was lying, Macaulay began to put him through what Doherty described as "the third degree." FitzGerald continued to protest that he was an American citizen. Father Power, who had been pacing up and down, barely able to contain his anger, came to the unfortunate brother's rescue. He cried out, in what Doherty recalled as "bass stentorian tones that I can still hear, 'He *is* an American citizen!'"

Macaulay was taken aback, but only momentarily. He then turned his attention to Doherty, who, as the son of a federal cabinet minister, was the most high-profile student there. The twenty-year-old had been shaken by Brother FitzGerald's interrogation, and had difficulty responding to Macaulay's rapid-fire questioning. He even hesitated when asked his age. Doherty didn't get the chance to explain that, religious exemptions aside, he had been declared medically unfit for military service.

By the time Macaulay finished his interviews, he'd determined that at least thirty-six of the Novitiate's people were

suspects as conscription evaders. Because he lacked transportation to take them all to Guelph, he arrested only three:
George Nunan, a youth with the suspiciously German-
sounding name of Schmidt and Marcus Doherty. He said
he'd return for the others in the morning.

The three students, who quite likely had never been in any
kind of legal trouble in their lives, were told to go to their
rooms and get whatever belongings they might require, and
then report back to Macaulay for the trip to town. Doherty
had packed a bag and was on his way down the stairs when
he encountered Father Quirk. The priest stopped him and
asked, "Marcus, does your father know about this?"

Doherty asked Bourque if he could call his father in
Ottawa. Bourque replied that they would have to get permission from "the officer in tweeds." Macaulay, still comporting
himself like a martinet, told Doherty he had ten minutes in
which to get a call through to the justice minister, and then,
"you come to the barracks."

Macaulay might well have thought that, because of the
late hour, the senior Doherty would be difficult to reach.
But Marcus got his father on the phone and explained what
was happening. A somewhat upset Charles Doherty told
his son to call Macaulay to the phone. It took only a brief
conversation to convince Doherty that Macaulay didn't
understand the nature of the religious exemption clause
and was carrying out an illegal investigation. Doherty told
Macaulay to remain at the Novitiate until he heard from a
superior officer.

It was now past midnight, and the telephone wires linking
Guelph, Ottawa and London hummed with a flurry of calls
that dragged high-ranking officers out of their beds. Justice
Minister Doherty reached the Adjutant General, Major

General Ernest Charles Ashton, and expressed his opinion that Captain Macaulay's actions were illegal, and he should withdraw his squad from the Novitiate. Ashton telephoned Major Hirsch in London, and then Macaulay. He told the captain to retire for the night, return to the Novitiate in the morning for further discussion with Father Bourque, and then submit a full report.

Macaulay, the military police squad and Inspector Menard returned to Guelph empty-handed. The young men who had briefly been under arrest went back to their own beds, relieved that they wouldn't have to spend the night in the barracks. The "Guelph Novitiate Raid" was over. But the trouble it engendered was just beginning.

The following morning Macaulay returned to the Novitiate to talk to Father Bourque. Whatever was said between the two men resulted in the rector writing a letter of protest to General Mewburn. "I will not accept the base imputation that this Religious Community is in league with deserters to evade the law, nor can I tolerate in the least degree that such an odious impression be made on the public mind as undoubtedly must be made [by] such a preposterous display of force."

Mewburn replied with a letter expressing his "deep regret" over Macaulay's actions. However, once the story became public, it touched off a storm of controversy. Guelph was at the centre of the tempest, but the winds of anger and religious acrimony spread to other Canadian communities.

Newspaper publishers across the country, including those in Guelph, who had cooperated with the government ban, were furious that the Toronto *Star* had been allowed to get away with an exclusive scoop. Because of their angry complaints, the government's Chief Censor,

E.J. Chambers, sought increased powers of enforcement. His office was granted the right to punish violators with stiff fines and prison terms of up to five years. Meanwhile, Catholic and Protestant spokesmen alike condemned the publication ban. The Protestants claimed that it reflected the influence of Catholic officials like Doherty, and protected the students at the Novitiate, including his own son. Reverend Spence referred to such censorship as "Kaiserism." The Catholics argued that the ban only left the Jesuits open to malicious slander.

General Mewburn, Major Hirsch and Father Bourque were all criticized for mishandling the Novitiate situation, but the bulk of official blame fell on Captain Macaulay. He and his men had been in civilian clothes, he hadn't produced written authority, and contrary to orders he had conducted himself in a high-handed manner. Moreover, Macaulay's own version of the events of that night didn't stand up to scrutiny.

Macaulay said he had considered all of the students to be suspects because they didn't produce the certificates proving exemption that were required under a recently passed order-in-council. But Reverend Joseph Bergin, the school's Professor of Classics, said no one had been asked to show the certificates. Had Macaulay requested them, they were readily available, because Father Bourque had given them to all the students. He'd instructed the young men not to set foot off the Novitiate property without the certificates, because he'd become aware of the bitter feelings of some Guelph residents.

If Macaulay had been properly briefed before the raid, or even if he'd arrived at the Novitiate in uniform with written authority, and approached Father Bourque in a respectful manner, he would have learned that several students weren't Canadian. Six, including Brother FitzGerald, were American. One was from England, and another from Poland.

The Canadian students were from New Brunswick, Quebec, Manitoba and Ontario. Three of them were Guelphites, and two (including Andrew Schmidt) were from the nearby town of Arthur. That any of them, regardless of province of origin, should be subject to a military police investigation, was regarded in Quebec as a petty persecution of the Jesuits motivated by hostile feelings toward Quebec. The story of Macaulay's uncivil manner with Father Bourque, a French Canadian, fuelled Quebecois suspicions. Captain Macaulay was soon transferred to a posting in Winnipeg, where members of the local Orange Lodge welcomed him as a hero. Ironically, Father Bourque was also transferred to Winnipeg, to be rector of St. Paul's College at the University of Manitoba.

Lieutenant Colonel H.A. Machin, Director of the Military Service Branch of the Ministry of Justice, and an Anglican, strongly denounced the Novitiate Raid. He referred to it as evidence that "a powerful cabal exists at Ottawa against the Minister of Justice." Machin went so far as to call those responsible for the raid "worse than the Huns." Then he stirred up sectarian animosity when he said that "the greatest menace in the province of Ontario at this time is the Methodist Church, which seeks to make us the most hypocritical province in Canada."

Machin's outburst embarrassed Doherty, and the Colonel eventually had to retract his comment. But it wasn't the end of accusations fired across religious lines. While the Jesuits considered taking legal action against "certain Protestant clergymen in Guelph," and even discussed the option of requesting the Pope to rule on whether or not their honour had been impugned, Father Power placed the cause of the trouble at the door of "clerical firebrands who do not represent the best elements of the Protestant community of Guelph."

Power mentioned no names, but his "firebrands" undoubtedly included Reverends Palmer and Spence. Palmer had been particularly outspoken about what he considered favouritism from Doherty's office toward Catholics. From his own pulpit, and those of churches in nearby communities like Preston and Fergus, Palmer delivered a speech that soon found its way into the *Orange Sentinel*:

> And now, brethren, I come to what to me is the crowning act of shame on the part of some people in our own district. Outside the city of Guelph, as some of you are aware, is the Novitiate of the Roman Catholic Church governed by the Jesuits. For many months past . . . persistent rumours were abroad that many young men, whose people were well off enough to pay the price, could be found there in hiding from military service. For a long time, some few of us in Guelph who believe in the principles 'Equal rights to all — special privileges to none' have been urging the military authorities to act and find out if there was any justification to the rumours.

In his conclusion, Palmer insisted that he demanded fairness for all young men; rich or poor, Roman Catholic or Protestant. But he also emphasized that one of those "hiding" was the son of a cabinet minister. It was already a matter of record that Marcus Doherty had been rejected as medically unfit for military service.

Palmer found a receptive audience for his speech in the Western Congregational Church in Toronto. He was applauded when he said that every fit young man of military age should be in uniform. When he said that the Jesuits had long been a power in Guelph, a voice from the pews cried, "Too long, sir!"

Palmer asked his audience, "Who is the government?"

Someone replied, "Doherty!"

When Palmer asked, "Who is governing the country today?" the same voice replied, "The Pope!"

During the "crisis," reporters from big city newspapers flocked to Guelph. Their stories on the Novitiate Raid and the political storm it had whipped up shared front pages with reports from the battlefields of Europe. When it became clear that, as far as the government was concerned, no laws had been broken and no one would be arrested, the visiting newsmen left town. But Guelph was still a hotbed of malicious rumours. One story claimed that a Jesuit priest had provided a falsified birth certificate for the son of a Catholic mother who needed "proof" that her boy was too young to be conscripted.

A rumour that made the front page in Guelph "added to the high pitch of excitement in the controversy between the Protestant Ministers and the heads of the Novitiate." Not far from the Novitiate, on the banks of the Speed River, the Jesuits owned a small forested lot with a bungalow they called the Villa. Guelph's gossip mill concocted a story that the priests were using the Villa as a hideout for more conscription-evading students. The Jesuits insisted that the Villa was used only as a summer retreat.

Controversy over the Novitiate Raid would continue until a Royal Commission hearing in September 1919, when the war was over and the case was no longer of great importance. The Commission concluded that the Jesuit students had been legally exempt from conscription. Most of the blame for the embarrassing affair fell on Captain Macaulay. Nonetheless, he was in some measure a scapegoat for an unfortunate incident that was rooted in misunderstanding, poor communications and the politics of religious intolerance.

Nursing sister Alice Trusdale survived the horrors of the front only to succumb to illness while treating soldiers back home in Canada. (Waterford Heritage & Agricultural Museum)

CHAPTER 10
UNSUNG HEROES AND ANGELS OF MERCY

"Real Nurses Wanted at the Front" the Guelph paper announced in its edition for December 29, 1914. The accompanying article described how in the Boer War, the poorly trained, amateur medical staff in British army hospitals were so incompetent that a story circulated about a wounded soldier who put a placard saying "Too sick to be nursed today" on the wall above his bed. The article quoted a trained nurse who said, "If Lord Kitchener had asked for 500,000 nurses to enlist instead of 500,000 men, he would have had the number the next morning."

The Canadian Army Medical Corps didn't want to repeat the errors of the past. The call went out for physicians, surgeons and nurses to put aside their private practices and hospital positions, and go overseas. Even more than the young men who felt duty-bound to "do their bit," medical practitioners were compelled by professional obligation to go where their services were most needed. As the war dragged on and the number of casualties and cases of sickness mounted at an alarming rate, the need for medical staff reached levels of desperation. Over the course of the war, more than half of the 7,472 doctors registered in Canada in 1914 served overseas; working in military hospitals in England and France, in dressing stations at the front and in field hospitals within the sound — and range — of enemy artillery. Of the more than 3,000 nursing sisters in the Canadian Army Medical Corps, over 2,500 did overseas duty. Among Guelph's medical people who answered the call were doctors Richard A. Ireland, and Ernest and Clarence Young; and nursing sisters Alice Trusdale and Sarah S. Livingstone.

The army's need for a legion of men and women to staunch at least some of the bleeding on the Western Front created yet another crisis at home: a shortage of doctors and trained nurses. In communities like Guelph, doctors who remained at home had to look after the patients of those who had gone to war. In an era when doctors still went out into the community to tend to the sick and injured and assist with births, the workload could be overwhelming. Patients, for their part, had to make the adjustment of placing themselves in the care of a new doctor with whom they were unfamiliar, and who, under the circumstances, might not always be available for house calls.

Very often, "Doctor Mother" tended to sick children in the absence of a physician. She made mustard plasters to treat congestion, eased the pain of sore throats with honey and hot lemon drinks and applied rubber hot water bottles to stop ear ache. Home remedies were sometimes the only option, with so much of the country's production of medicines and ointments drawn off by the war, and medications formerly imported from Europe becoming ever scarcer.

The pages of the newspapers were full of advertisements for "medicines" of dubious quality and mysterious ingredients whose manufacturers claimed would cure everything from constipation to consumption.

Like all Canadian health care institutions, Guelph's hospitals had to adjust to functioning with skeleton staffs bolstered by volunteers from the public, as doctors, nurses and even not-yet-graduated students from medical schools went into military service. The shortage of doctors in Canada was so acute that some medical students serving overseas were sent home to complete their studies. With the coming of conscription, medical students would be exempted from compulsory military service. An article from the December 6, 1915 issue of the local paper tells how the Guelph Homewood Sanitarium was "hard hit" by the war. Four of the institution's doctors, one of whom was Richard Ireland, were "with the colors."

It wasn't only the loss of the doctors that contributed to what the paper called an "acute problem" at the Homewood. A hospital spokesman said, "Right at the outbreak of the war two of our firemen [furnace operators], who were naval reservists, left right off the bat, and others have been going ever since. I guess we must have at least 35 or more men at the front."

Among the other employees who left to "join the battle" were the Homewood's painter and chief cook. Finding replacements for them was almost as difficult as filling the vacancies left by the doctors because, as one anonymous Homewood official told the newspaper, "So many able-bodied men are leaving the country, that it affects all the number of men available."

Of the Homewood's medical staff, Dr. Clifford M. Keillor served with the British army at the Dardanelles. Dr. Ernest Z. Stirrett became chief surgeon on HMCS *Niobe*, and died of illness in June 1917. Doctors Harold H. Argue and Richard Ireland both served in France. Ireland would be one of the Homewood's — and Guelph's — unsung heroes.

A native of Trenton, Ontario, Ireland had studied medicine at the University of Toronto, graduating in 1911. Like many of the other students there, he'd belonged to a militia regiment. After working as a house surgeon at Toronto General Hospital, he'd moved to Newfoundland and started a private practice in St. John's. He'd left there to take the position of chief house surgeon at the Homewood.

In the summer of 1915, Ireland was appointed Medical Officer of the 76th Battalion. He was one of the doctors who examined recruits and decided whether or not they were physically fit for military service. It was an essential duty that could have kept Ireland in Canada for the duration of the war. But, at twenty-seven, Ireland was in the same age group as most of the eager young men he certified as fit for duty. Ireland would have seen the obituaries of slain Guelph soldiers, some of whom he might have personally met. He decided that he was needed more at the front than at the Homewood or a recruiting station. In January 1916, he joined the Canadian Army Medical Corps with the rank of captain. He sailed for England in April.

Ireland served with a field ambulance unit during the Battle of the Somme and at Vimy Ridge. By autumn of 1917 he was senior medical officer with the Canadian Mounted Rifles. On October 30, during the Passchendaele campaign, Ireland was at the front treating wounded men in a pillbox, a concrete structure that had been converted into an aid station. The pillbox was soon filled to capacity, so stretcher-bearers had to put the overflow of wounded on the ground outside. Ireland left the protection of the pillbox to tend to the men lying out in the open. While he was performing his duties, he was killed by an exploding artillery shell. Guelphites read in the local paper that Dr. Ireland had been killed in France, but the details of his heroism were buried in unpublicized military reports.

William and Frances Young of Guelph had three sons who were doctors: Ernest, William Jr. and Clarence. Ernest was on the medical staff at the Hospital for the Insane in London, Ontario. He became the assistant superintendent and gained a reputation as one of the most brilliant doctors in his field in Ontario. Clarence had taken a position as physician and surgeon for the Western Section of the Grand Trunk Railway. His patients were railroad employees, passengers and people who lived in isolated locations along the line. William Jr. had established a private practice in Elmira, a small community not far from Guelph.

In the spring of 1916, Ernest joined the Canadian Army Medical Corps. Clarence went to England, where he volunteered for the Royal Army Medical Corps. Both brothers were soon wading in the blood of front-line casualty stations, fighting to save lives while the world around them shook from artillery bombardments.

On the morning of November 1, 1916, a telegram was delivered to the Young home on Edinburgh Road in Guelph. Like many of their neighbours who also had family members overseas, William and Frances had been living in dread of the telegram boy bearing terrible news. To their relief, the message was not a death notice from the government, but a brief exclamation of celebration from Ernest. It said, "Clarence gets military cross for conspicuous bravery. All well." Bursting with pride, William hurried downtown to show the telegram to the newspaper editors. The news of a Guelph-born doctor being decorated appeared in that evening's edition.

Because Dr. Clarence Young had been awarded the Military Cross, reports of his action of "conspicuous gallantry and devotion to duty" weren't shuffled away into military files to be forgotten. Guelphites eventually learned through the paper that Young's aid post had been attacked and almost surrounded, and most of the officers killed or injured. Under heavy enemy fire, Young successfully evacuated many wounded men. "His energy and disregard for his personal safety inspired all who came in contact with him," the citation said. "He tended the wounded under heavy fire, displaying great courage and determination." The Military Cross was a prestigious award, even more so when, as in Dr. Clarence Young's case, it was accompanied by a Bar. The medal ranked third in stature after the Victoria Cross and the Distinguished Service Order. The recipient was entitled to use the post-nominal letters MC. Young's medal was an object of pride not only for his family, but also for his hometown. The paper always reported glowingly when Guelph men received such honours. It reflected well on the city, and could even inspire men who had not yet enlisted to report to the recruiting station. Guelphites would recall Dr. Young's moment of glory a few years later, under different circumstances.

Guelph nurses were also "doing their bit." The Guelph General Hospital had a nursing school that attracted students from all over Wellington and nearby counties. Graduate nurses often stayed on at the General and became Guelph residents. One was Sarah Sterling Livingstone, originally from Halton County. She was a familiar figure at the hospital and was well known in the city. At age thirty-three and single, Livingstone decided in July 1916 to follow the example of so many of her colleagues and volunteer for the Canadian Army Medical Corps. A few months later, newspaper readers learned of a poignant encounter between the Guelph nurse and a wounded Guelph soldier.

On November 18, 1916, Private John "Jack" Lovering was struck in the hand by shrapnel. Lovering and his younger brother Charles had enlisted within a week of each other. One month before Jack was wounded, Charles had been killed. In mid-December, Lovering's sister, Mrs. Wilfrid Cook of Suffolk Street, received a short letter from Jack, written in a Canadian army hospital in France and dated November 26. The handwriting was not Jack's:

> My Dear Sister — I am fairly comfortable here, but I hope to get home to Canada. I have lost two fingers and part of the back of my right hand. I hope to hear from you soon. Your loving brother, Jack.

The letter was accompanied by another note:

> Dear Mrs. Cook — I have been the night nurse in charge of the ward where your brother is for three weeks. He has been here about two days. His hand is doing nicely, but he seems to have a very bad cold. However, we hope he will be better soon. At present he talks a great deal while sleeping and does not seem to rest well. I am a Guelph nurse and shall try to give your brother every comfort. Am very busy tonight, so will not write more. Sincerely Yours, S.S. Livingstone.

> [PS] Your brother asked me to write for him. S.L.

Lovering's "very bad cold" was pneumonia. He died the following day. The telegram bearing the news of his death would have reached his sister's home well in advance of the letter. Perhaps his sister took some solace in learning that Jack had someone from home at his bedside during his last hours.

Alice Louise Trusdale, known to family and friends as Allie, was from Waterford, Ontario. She became a nursing student at the Guelph General Hospital, graduating with honours in 1912. For the next two years she was a nurse on the hospital's staff. Then the war started.

Trusdale went to London where she enlisted in the Canadian Army Medical Corps. After a year of training, Lieutenant Trusdale was sent overseas. Like Sarah Livingstone, Trusdale witnessed the horrors of the army hospitals, where antibiotics were yet unknown and anaesthetics were in short supply. She would no doubt have wearily nodded in agreement with the Nursing Sister who told a journalist, "I was put in the operating room and we three girls had 291 operations in ten nights, so that will give you an idea of a week's work."

Like Sarah Livingstone and other "Bluebirds" and "Angels of Mercy," as the soldiers called them, Trusdale comforted dying young men for whom she could do little more than hold their hands. To lift her own spirits, she might well have joined with her colleagues in singing, "My Sweet Little Alice Blue Gown." It went, in part:

> In my sweet little Alice Blue gown
> When I first came to Birmingham town
> I had a bad trip in a nasty old ship
> And the cold in my billet just gave me the pip
> We came out to nurse our own troops
> But were greeted with measles and whoops

Now I'll be a granny and sit on my fanny
And keep warm with turpentine stupes

By the war's end, extra lines had been added:

I was happy and gay to have served with
McCrae
In my sweet little Alice Blue gown

Six Canadian nursing sisters were killed when a military hospital in France was bombed. Fourteen were lost when a German U-boat torpedoed the Canadian hospital ship *Llandovery Castle*, and then machine-gunned survivors of the sinking in their lifeboats. Other nursing sisters were carried off by sickness. Allie Trusdale would eventually return to Guelph, putting France behind her, but not the war.

In the meantime, the residents of Guelph learned to get by with fewer doctors and nurses, just as hospitals adjusted to the shortage of people to work as firemen, cooks and custodial and maintenance staff. It was all considered part of the national sacrifice necessary for victory. There were even unexpected developments that at the time were perceived as silver linings in the war's dark cloud.

A spokesman for the Homewood told the paper of a young man who was a patient there, without mentioning the nature of the problem for which he was being treated. With his doctors and other Homewood staff leaving to go to war, the patient begged his mother for her permission to enlist. She gave in, and the young man was soon in the trenches. He was wounded in action and sent back home to Guelph. The Homewood spokesman told the reporter, "The war made a man of him."

War as a marketing theme. The ad at top promotes smoking to relieve tedium "in war and peace." The ad at bottom offers cash prizes for finding soldiers' faces hidden in the war puzzle. (Guelph Mercury)

CHAPTER 11

"IT'S A HAPPY TRENCH THAT HAS BLACK CATS IN IT"

"Said Farewell to Store Mates Who Leave for Front" announced a headline of November 18, 1914. The article was about a banquet held by management and male staff members of D.E. Macdonald and Bros. Ltd., one of Guelph's largest department stores. They were honouring employees Will Cotton and Fred Letheren, who had volunteered for military service and were about to embark for the army base near London. Most of the column space was taken up with the text of a lengthy address delivered by Mr. C. Meadows, who spoke on behalf of the staff.

Meadows's speech reflected the giddy atmosphere of patriotism that had taken hold in Guelph during those early days of the war. Cotton and Letheren were among the first to step forward for the grand adventure:

You are both going to serve your King and Country — a most noble errand and one that we have not the slightest doubt you will carry out creditably. The life of a soldier is by no means a bed of roses, particularly in war time, and the man who goes forth at this juncture deserves far greater praise than the tongue of man can accord.

Meadows went on to say that the four most profound words the young men should look to for guidance in difficult times were *honesty, sobriety, industry* and *obedience*. He told them, "Be always painstaking in all you undertake to do. Never grumble — always have a kind word for your comrades, and should it fall to your lot to go forward to the firing line, face the enemy fearlessly."

The splendid send-off Macdonald and Bros. gave two war-bound employees was not uncommon in the optimism of 1914. The same issue that carried the Cotton and Letheren story also had a shorter article about Albert Finch, an employee of the Queen's Hotel. When his employers learned he had enlisted, they hastily organized an event. "We are sorry to part with an old friend," the obligatory speech went, "one who all along has proved himself a good old sport."

The downtown core, with its grey limestone buildings, three and four storeys high, was Guelph's economic nerve centre. Department stores, pharmacies, banks, restaurants, dry goods stores, tobacconists and other businesses employed scores of young men whose faces were as familiar to downtown shoppers as those of their own families. Charles Kerse, Charles McGowan, Frederick Bond, Paul Grant and others would soon be in uniform.

Scattered throughout the city were neighbourhood grocery stores, bakeries and butcher shops, most of them family operations. The proprietors' sons made home deliveries. Youths like Robert Davis, George Lowe and Austin Thomas, who had hauled groceries in wagons and sleds, joined the lines of volunteers. Their leaving tore the human fabric of their neighbourhoods.

From the beginning, the war provided merchants with opportunities to mix patriotism with business. Flags, bunting and recruiting posters decorated shop windows. Union Jack parasols cost twenty-five cents. At the E.J. Patrick Furniture Mart, Guelphites could buy "life-like" photographs of "Campaign Heroes" such as British Secretary of State for War Lord Kitchener, Field Marshall John French and Admiral John Jellicoe of the Royal Navy. By November, Patrick's had a "Big War Map" on display in the front window. It was updated every morning so passersby could keep track of the movements of armies on the Western Front — and, hopefully, step inside to buy something. At the J.D. McCarthur Shoe Store, customers could buy fashionable military footwear like Ames Holden McCready boots, the very ones chosen by a parliamentary commission for the Canadian army. Some Guelph merchants accepted war bonds as currency.

Merchants enhanced their newspaper advertisements with war-related themes. They used militaristic terminology like *drive, countersign*, and *follow the flag*. The Royal City Shoe Store announced a "Great Bombardment" sale. D.E. Macdonald ran an ad that said, "In These Difficult Times Every Store Has a Patriotic Duty to Perform." D.E. Macdonald's "patriotic duty" was to protect customers from unnecessary price increases. The ad's artwork featured an army bugler. He was dressed in the uniform and pith helmet of a nineteenth-century British soldier, and looked more like a trooper from the Boer War than a Tommy in the trenches of France. The romantic, outdated image was just one small indication of the prevailing misconceptions of the war.

Slick corporate advertising focused on war and patriotism. The Black Cat cigarette company ran a series of ads that featured its trademark mascot, a human-sized black cat, in a variety of militaristic settings. In one, the cat wears an officer's sword and offers cigarettes to soldiers in a trench while shells burst in the background. The caption reads, "It's a Happy Trench that has Black Cats in it. All kinds of tedium may be relieved by a really good smoke — 'Trench Duty,' either in war or peace, is made less irksome by smoking."

By sending thirty coupons from cigarette packages to Black Cat Headquarters in Montreal, members of the "Black Cat Army" would receive one of the company's new war games. According to the ads, these games were not only entertaining, but also taught valuable lessons about geography and the strategies and tactics of war.

Although tobacco use was widespread at that time, some people considered it a vice, if not a health hazard. There was no such taboo on chewing gum. The makers of Wrigley's gum ran ads with images that alternated between gum-chewing children and soldiers. Spearmint, Doublemint and Juicy Fruit were advertised as being good for the teeth and the stomach. Wrigley's was promoted as the preferred gum of the land forces and the fleet. "Wrigley's gives solace in the long watch, it freshens and refreshens, steadies nerves, allays thirst." The ads urged parents of soldiers to "Keep your boy at the front supplied."

As the months passed and the hard reality of the war increasingly became a fact of daily life, people in Guelph might well have wondered if there was a company that *didn't* use the conflict and the plight of the men in the trenches to plug products. The manufacturer of the Auto-Strop Safety Razor noted in its ads that "Every soldier shaves under difficulties — cold water, chilling atmosphere and a time allowance of about three minutes . . . The Auto-Strop overcomes all shaving difficulties . . . Give him an Auto-Strop — the gift of the hour."

"These are Anxious Days" was the lead for another ad. "Never in the history of this old world have the people lived under such tremendous strain as today. Millions awake each morning in fearful dread of what the day may bring forth, and live each hour with nerves at the highest tension."

The ad went on to describe the wonderful effects of Dr. Chase's Nerve Food. If your favourite store in Guelph didn't have it in stock, it was available by mail from Toronto for just fifty cents a box.

The Victor Talking Machine Company had already introduced the world to its iconic trademark mascot, a dog peering into a gramophone horn, listening for "His Master's Voice." Now the ads featured a soldier carrying a rifle with fixed bayonet, charging through smoke and barbed wire. The ad for Scott's Emulsion (a brand of cod liver oil) told parents, "The abrupt change from home comforts to camp may be trying on your boy's health." All the lad had to do was take this "rich liquid food" to enjoy richer blood, body warmth and fortified lungs and throat.

The Kellogg's Company promoted Corn Flakes as a replacement for bread in "patriotic meals" because, "Our armies and allies need every pound of wheat we can spare them." Kellogg's secured an endorsement from the office of the federal Food Controller in Ottawa, which was published in their newspaper ads.

The Ford Motor Company ran ads that explained how their cars increased food production for the war effort. "It has been estimated that five acres of land are required to maintain one horse for a year, and that the same five acres would produce enough food for two people. If 50,000 Canadian farmers each replaced one horse with a Ford, 250,000 acres would be added to the Nation's source of food supply."

The Lever Bros. Company, makers of Sunlight Soap, introduced Sunlight Sue. Ads showed Sue sitting on a couch, knitting. Because she used Sunlight laundry soap, Sue had all of her washing done by 10 a.m., and therefore had plenty of time to knit socks for the soldiers in the trenches.

The Good Hope Manufacturing Company of Montreal offered cash prizes and "Many Merchandise Prizes" to people who could solve the war puzzle it placed in newspapers. The puzzle was an illustration of a tank rolling across no man's land with artillery shells bursting around it. The challenge was to find the eleven soldiers' faces camouflaged into the picture.

As a result of dairy shortages, ads appeared for *oleomargarine*. This early form of margarine, made principally from vegetable oils and water, had been around since the mid-nineteenth century, but had been banned in Canada through the efforts of the dairy industry. The ban was lifted in 1917, and the product was promoted as "The Great Substitute for Butter." Yellow food-colouring disguised its unappetizing, lard-like appearance. It represented a sacrifice of sorts at the family table.

Promotional campaigns such as the *Dollar Day–Mystery Man* collaboration between downtown merchants and the local paper gave residents a respite from the daily anxieties of the war. The whole city was caught up in the combination retail bargain sale and contest. The downtown core had an almost festive atmosphere as crowds filled the streets and people tried to identify the "Mercury Mystery Man" for a cash reward. Stories of the Mystery Man's adventures shared the front page with news from the Western Front.

Large companies and local merchants eventually toned down the jingoistic war themes in their advertising. Dissatisfaction was festering, over the manner in which the war had been managed — or botched. People became more likely to see plain ads, such as one for Guelph's Neil the Shoe Man informing them of a "War Economy Sale." War shortages that affected almost every form of commodity or merchandise resulted in ads such as one by Kelly's Music Store in Guelph, informing patrons, that for the first time in two years, they had received a shipment of gramophone needles.

Fred Letheren and Will Cotton would eventually come home. Charles Kerse, Charles McGowan, Frederick Bond, Robert Davis, George Lowe and Austin Thomas were among the many who would not. Others would come back permanently disabled. The war had laid a dark hand, both on many Guelph homes, and on the shops and other businesses in which so many young men had been employed.

Three boys pose with the bust of Kaiser Wilhelm I on August 24, 1914. They had "rescued" the bust after vandals dumped it in the lake in Victoria Park in Berlin, Ontario. In a controversial referendum, the city's name was changed to Kitchener. (Kitchener Public Library and Waterloo Historical Society)

CHAPTER 12
ANY NAME BUT BERLIN

John Alexander Ferguson of Berlin, Ontario, might have been deliberately avoiding attention from the press when on February 10, 1915, he went to the recruiting office in Guelph to volunteer for the CEF. Although he'd grown up in Berlin and was a member of a Waterloo County militia unit, Ferguson had been born in Eramosa. But it probably wasn't his Wellington County roots that compelled Ferguson to sign up in Guelph instead of Berlin. A few months earlier, Ferguson had been a central figure in a dramatic incident that touched off a stormy period in Berlin.

Berlin was known as Canada's "German capital." Though it was named after the capital city of Germany, it had actually been founded by German-speaking Mennonites from Pennsylvania — the "Pennsylvania Dutch" — who came north seeking cheap land after the American Revolution. Later, many immigrants from Germany chose Berlin as the place to settle.

By the summer of 1914, Berlin was a city of about twenty thousand. It had German clubs, publications and theatrical and musical societies. The German language was taught in schools. But the community's "Germanness," long a source of local pride, now placed it in an uncomfortable situation.

At the beginning of the war, a handful of immigrants in Berlin who were reservists of the German army went to the German consulate in Toronto before it closed down so they could offer their services to the Kaiser. A few other Berliners openly sympathized with the German cause. But they were the exception. The great majority of ethnic German residents were patriotic Canadian citizens. Moreover, as the seventh largest industrial centre in Ontario, Berlin stood to see its economy bolstered by lucrative government war contracts, so there were pragmatic incentives for patriotism.

In churches where services were conducted in German, clergymen led their congregations in declaring loyalty to Canada and the king. German Berliners followed the advice of the *Berliner Journal*, which counselled, "Be silent, and face these hard times with dignity." They could love the old country, the newspaper said, without betraying the country that was their home.

The British government attempted to pressure the Canadian federal government into arresting all German and Austrian reservists in Canada. Prime Minister Borden refused, stating that they were loyal Canadians who were "entitled to the protection of the law and would receive it."

They would not be interfered with unless they attempted to aid the enemy.

However, Berlin became a focal point in the wave of anti-German sentiment that swept across Canada with the spread of stories about atrocities the Kaiser's army had inflicted upon Belgium's civilian population. The teaching of German in schools was suspended. Amidst swirling rumours of enemy agents, suspicion fell upon German immigrants and Canadians with German-sounding names. No community in Canada had more of both than Berlin. Some ethnic Germans chose to "fit in" by anglicizing their names. *Schmidt*, for example, became *Smith*, or the prefix *von* was dropped. German-language newspapers were scrutinized for anything that might be considered pro-German or anti-British. Even so, they joined English-language newspapers in protesting the censorship of war news. They also advised their readers that reports from the Western Front that did get through the censors came from biased British and French sources. Only through newspapers published in the neutral United States did information from (equally biased) German sources filter into Canada.

In the patriotic fervour of the war's early days, long before any Canadian soldier fired a shot in anger or fell in battle, some non-German Berlin residents decided they had to disassociate themselves from the Teutonic "Hun" culture around them. A few demonstrated their patriotism by publicly burning a German flag. But the act that caught national attention was an attack on an object that was suddenly considered a symbol of German imperialism and arrogance. It occupied a place of honour in the middle of Berlin.

In 1897, a bronze (or copper) bust of Kaiser Wilhelm I (grandfather of Wilhelm II) had been unveiled in Berlin's

Victoria Park in a grand ceremony presided over by the mayor and the German consul from Toronto. Imported from Germany, the bust depicted a stern-faced Kaiser wearing a spiked Prussian military helmet. The sculpture was about four feet high, weighed over 150 pounds and was perched on a six-foot granite pedestal ironically called the Peace Memorial, which rested on a four-foot-high base. Secured to the sides of the pedestal were two large bronze medallions that featured the likenesses of German Chancellor Otto Von Bismarck and Prussian General Helmuth Von Moltke. The total cost of the monument, $1,186, had been covered by donations from all over Waterloo County, as well as from neighbouring communities, including Guelph.

The bust had a prominent place overlooking the lake in Victoria Park. However, the Kaiser took a secondary place to Queen Victoria in 1911, when a larger-than-life statue of the late British monarch was unveiled nearby. Wilhelm I remained in Victoria's shadow until the weekend of August 23–24, 1914.

Sometime between nightfall on Saturday and dawn on Sunday, someone crept into the deserted park, tied a rope around the Kaiser's neck, and hauled the bust off its pedestal. The Kaiser was found Sunday morning, stuck head-first in the mud at the bottom of the shallow lake. Three teenage boys donned swimming costumes and helped carry out a rescue operation. The bust was turned over to the Concordia Society for safekeeping in their club rooms above the Grand Theatre.

German Berliners were outraged by the act of vandalism. Mayor W.D. Euler said that German Canadians were loyal citizens, and the attack on the Kaiser's bust would only increase local tensions. He had a night guard placed in the park to prevent further vandalism of the pedestal and any retaliatory defacing of the statue of Queen Victoria.

Three days later the police arrested John Ferguson and his pals Fred Bolton and Alan Smith, ages seventeen to twenty. The youths confessed to the crime. Ferguson admitted to climbing up the pedestal and putting the rope around the Kaiser's neck. They were charged with vandalism, but it doesn't seem they were ever sentenced or made to pay for damages.

The incident was well-covered by the press, and not all Canadians saw it as a crime. Why, after all, should a monument to the grandfather of the reigning German tyrant have a distinguished place in a Canadian park, next to a statue of the British Empire's beloved queen? To many Canadians, especially non-Germans in Berlin, Ferguson and his friends were patriotic young men who had removed a foreign blight from a public place, and deserved to be commended.

Within days, Bolton and Smith headed for Valcartier to enlist. Five months passed before Ferguson slipped over to Guelph to follow their example. In that time, there had been some unfortunate developments in Berlin.

A German-born Lutheran clergyman and philosophy professor named Carl Tappert was accused of being pro-German for questioning the veracity of propaganda about "Hun" atrocities. Soldiers took delight in disrupting his Sunday services. He would eventually be forced to leave town after being dragged from his home and beaten up. Some ethnic German businessmen had their shops broken into and robbed of such seditious items as German flags and pictures of the Kaiser. A major sore point was the fact that Berlin lagged well behind other communities in recruiting. Smaller cities like Guelph boasted many more volunteers. Recruiting officers suspected that some of the "fit" young men of Berlin who refused to enlist were just slackers who were willing to sit back and let others do the fighting; every community had its share of those. But in the case of Berlin, the officers were sure that most of the ethnic German males of military age not in uniform were secretly "Hun" sympathizers.

Berlin men who had already enlisted harassed other youths on King Street, the main downtown thoroughfare, even dragging them bodily to the recruiting station. They browbeat the young men's female companions for not encouraging them to be "real men" and enlist. One victimized couple turned out to be American visitors.

The trouble reached a peak on the evening of February 15. A mob of forty to fifty soldiers, their anger fuelled by alcohol, attacked the headquarters of the Concordia Society. They kicked the doors open, poured in and emerged with their prize, the bust of Kaiser Wilhelm. Singing "Rule Britannia" and "God Save the King," the soldiers paraded through downtown Berlin, carrying the bust like a trophy of war. They stopped periodically to shout recruiting slogans.

With nary a police constable in sight, the soldiers returned to the Concordia Society headquarters and tore it apart. They shattered windows and splintered doors. Furniture, including a piano, was smashed to kindling and the pieces tossed into the street. The growing pile was soaked with gasoline and ignited. Onto the bonfire went tables, chairs, bar fixtures and ornaments, as well as decks of cards, German flags, German hymn books and photographs of German royalty. Committed to the flames with the latter was a photograph of King George V posing with a German flag.

Military officers finally arrived on the scene and took charge. The soldiers returned to their barracks, allegedly hauling the Kaiser's bust with them so they could use it for target practice. This time, it vanished for good.

By the spring of 1915, Canadian troops were in the trenches of the Western Front, and casualty reports began to appear in their hometown newspapers. Stories about Canadian valour contrasted with accounts of Hun villainy. Month after month, the press and the politicians increased the volume of anti-German rhetoric. Hatred for all things German grew. By early 1916, factory owners in Berlin were concerned that their city's name could damage business. They were doing very well with government war contracts, but feared a public boycott of anything "Made in Berlin" that would hurt sales of their domestic goods. The Berlin Board of Trade suggested that the city's name be changed.

The very idea was polarizing. Families that had been in the community for generations were proud of the name Berlin, and opposed any change. They pointed out that neighbouring communities like Bamberg, Breslau and New Hamburg had German names, and nobody was suggesting they change.

But the Board of Trade insisted that the name Berlin was an economic liability. Moreover, King George V himself was under pressure to change his family's name. Since the day of Queen Victoria's marriage to Prince Albert of Germany, the British royal family had belonged to the House of Saxe-Coburg and Gotha. Now Parliament was telling the king that the British people would be suspicious of a monarch with a German name. In 1917, George would denounce his grandfather's name in favour of the more suitably English surname of Windsor.

In Berlin, the proposed name change sparked heated arguments in city hall, and confrontations in the streets. The Berlin *News-Record* published satirical poems. One was titled "The Name."

> There's a city in Ontario
> And it's known far and near
> And the citizens are proud of it
> And its name they hold most dear.
>
> But now a cloud hangs over it
> And on its name a stain
> They tell us we must bury it
> With bitter tears and shame.

In a referendum held on May 19, 1916, 60 per cent of Berlin's eligible voters cast ballots. Those in favour of changing the name won by eighty-one votes. But a new name had yet to be chosen.

City council appointed a committee to prepare a list of possible names. The "short list" the committee presented was anything but. Among more than a hundred suggested names were: Eyelet City (for the shoe factories), Berfis (for the Allied nations of Belgium, England, Russia, France, Italy and Serbia), Bercana (for Berlin and Canada), Brock (for War of 1812 hero General Isaac Brock) and Loyal City (for obvious reasons). Other suggestions included King George, Hydro City, Khaki, Empire City, Progress, Factoria, Dawn and Uranus.

The list became a national joke. "No, dear reader, those are not characters in grand opera," quipped the Stratford *Beacon*. "They are Berlin's choice of names."

The Montreal *Star* said, "To be added to the minor horrors of war. Any of the patent names hitherto published as a substitute for Berlin, Ontario."

The Guelph paper asked, "Why under the sun didn't they put in Onions and Geraniums to fill out the list?"

While Canada laughed at Berlin's predicament, fate intervened. On June 5, 1916, Lord Horatio Herbert Kitchener, the British Secretary of State for War, was lost at sea when his ship struck a mine. Kitchener had been a national hero and a driving force behind the war effort. His image glared from recruiting posters throughout the British Empire. The sudden death of such an iconic figure was stunning. It seemed only fitting that his distinguished name be added to the list. In a second referendum held over four days in June, only 892 citizens turned out to vote for their choice from a list that had been pared down to six names. Kitchener won over second-place Brock by eleven votes. The "German capital of Canada" was officially renamed after a British imperialist.

The name change didn't end suspicions about German sympathies in the city. "Proof" of disloyalty came in October 1916 when a returned Guelph soldier named James Mills told the newspaper he had met a former Berlin man among a group of German PoWs. In January 1917, the discovery of some boxes of rifles and ammunition in a country school-house near Kitchener — described in the paper as a "School Arsenal" — sparked yet another rumour of a pro-German plot. But the Guelph paper couldn't be smug about the neighbouring city's problems.

Guelph also had a German name. When Queen Anne, the last British monarch of the Stuart dynasty, died without an heir in 1714, the crown went to her second cousin, George Guelph (or Gwelf), her nearest non-Catholic male relative. George was the ruler of the German principality of Hanover. He became King George I of Great Britain and Ireland. In 1827, during the reign of King George IV, John Galt founded the city that he named in honour of the royal family. Guelph was the name to which Queen Victoria was born.

However, the line of British monarchs that began with George I was always referred to as the Hanoverian dynasty. Although Guelphites proudly called their community "The Royal City," by 1914 not many Canadians would have been aware of the name's German origin. *Guelph* certainly didn't stand out as glaringly as *Berlin*. But the war nonetheless brought Guelph its own problem with a despised name.

In 1855, a small residential street in a new subdivision had been given the name Berlin. It was one of a cluster of streets named after Ontario communities, such as Elora, Galt, Preston and Fergus. Therefore, Berlin Street was not directly named for the German capital.

Soon after the war started, the question arose in city council as to whether a Guelph street should bear the name of the enemy capital. The paper said it was an "obnoxious German cognomen" which should be changed to "something more British sounding." Most of Berlin Street's residents objected to the idea. They didn't think the name of the street on which they'd grown up should be changed just because of a tyrannical Kaiser. The street had been named after the Canadian Berlin, not the German one.

Moreover, a name change would be impractical since residents' personal and official documentation bore the address Berlin Street. Nobody could even agree on what a new name should be. The war wouldn't last forever, the residents argued, so why not leave the name as it was? Some of them had men overseas. Mary Ryde of 77 Berlin Street had lost her son, William, in 1915.

City council debated the matter several times, but couldn't come to a decision. Then in 1916, neighbouring Berlin had its name changed to Kitchener. The Guelph street was no longer the namesake of a Canadian city. To the frustration of a growing number of Guelphites who considered the name unpatriotic, city council still didn't act.

In April 1917, the CEF won a spectacular victory at Vimy Ridge that captured the imagination of the entire country. Before long, a petition was being circulated in Guelph calling for Berlin Street to be renamed Vimy Avenue. One of the signatories was Thomas Foster, a former city fuel commissioner and a Berlin Street resident.

Changing the street's name still wasn't high on city council's list of priorities. The war effort had caused shortages of almost everything, especially money. Streets needed repairs. There was a drainage problem in St. Patrick's Ward. Organizations like the local chapter of the Red Cross were crying out for financial assistance. Mrs. C.W. Crowe, president of the Wellington County Red Cross Canning Kitchen, admonished the city finance committee:

> Not one of you aldermen has a son overseas.
> But surely you realize what we are trying to do
> for them. I have been told that money is not

available because you are repairing streets, but if it had not been for our boys overseas, the aldermen might have been fixing these streets themselves under German rule.

In the face of such demanding issues, city council repeatedly shoved the Berlin Street issue aside, even though letters to the editor, such as one signed "A Watcher," demanded to know, "Why does the name Berlin still disgrace one of Guelph's streets, and moreover, disgraces every British subject in Guelph?" The matter would not receive city council's full attention until late in the summer of 1918. By that time, the names of Guelph men killed overseas were appearing in the paper at an alarming rate.

The CEF was the spearhead of a major Allied offensive that had the German army reeling. One enemy strongpoint after another collapsed. The war's end was in sight, but ultimate victory was exacting a horrific toll. Losses struck households all over Guelph. Among the families to receive heartbreaking news that August were those of Vincent Bowen, Victor Henderson, Patrick Kelleher, John Mitchell, Wilfred Oakes, John Samuel, Carl Stickney and Percy Swift. The list for early September included the names of Frederick Kirvan, Percy Quarterman and Douglas Russell. Nobody doubted the list would grow.

In a bereaved community, city council finally had to act. On September 16, 1918, by a vote of nine to two, city council officially erased the name Berlin from the map of Guelph. But the street wasn't renamed Vimy Avenue. It became Foster Avenue, in recognition of Thomas Foster's years of civic service.

Less than two months later, the armistice of November 11 ended the fighting on the Western Front. Of the three young men who vandalized the bust of Kaiser Wilhelm I and then went off to fight his grandson, only two returned home. John Alexander Ferguson was shot dead by a sniper at Passchendaele on October 30, 1917.

This truck driver was one of the many women who contributed to the war effort by doing "men's work." (Courtesy of Guelph Museums 1969.48.69)

CHAPTER 13
SPARTAN MOTHERS AND WHITE FEATHERS

"Soldier's Wife Has Grievance" was the unusually bold-faced heading above a letter to the editor published on September 6, 1917. Also unusual was the subheading: "Slackers' Families Taunts of Charity Are Insulting." The letter went:

> To the Editor of the Mercury:
>
> Please allow me space in your paper to ask a few questions. When a woman's husband has been at the front ever since the beginning of the war, leaving a baby three months old, also four other children, I would like to know if the family of such a soldier are living on charity and is it to be allowed

that such things are to be thrown up by a neighbor who has neither husband or [sic] son fighting? If such is the case, the families of the soldiers would be very thankful if the Government would release their husbands and fathers, so it would not be possible for such insults to be thrown at them. Thanking you for this space, I am.

A SOLDIER'S WIFE

At that time it wasn't uncommon for authors of letters to the editor to withhold their names. In this case, the use of the word *Slackers* in the subheading indicates that the editor was firmly on the side of Soldier's Wife. Whoever she was, her letter provides a documentary window into the complex situation of Canadian women during the Great War. In this case, a mother had been socially criticized for allegedly "living on charity" while her husband was serving in the CEF. In turn, she rebuked the accusing neighbour "who has neither husband or son fighting."

Because she says her husband had been at the front since the beginning of the war, Soldier's Wife would have been among the thousands of married Canadian women who'd been obliged to make a difficult decision. In the early days of the war, a married man could not enlist without his wife's written consent. Considering the pressure placed on men by government and peers to do their duty for king and country, that regulation must have caused strife in many households in which wives were reluctant to comply. In what was still a patriarchal society, it would have been humiliating for a husband to have to say that he couldn't join the army because his wife wouldn't let him.

A wife's reluctance to let her husband go to war was understandable. Above all was the fear that he wouldn't come home. But there was also the pragmatic question of how she was to live while he was away. The dilemma was even greater for couples with children.

Soldiers' wives received an allotment of their husbands' pay, as well as a separation allowance from the government. If the man had given up a good-paying job, that money might still be insufficient. Should there be small children in the home, getting a job might not be a practical option for the mother. Some married soldiers solved the problem by having their wives and children move in with parents or other relations.

Men who were determined to enlist even without their wives' consent would declare themselves single or use false names when they filled out attestation papers. However, in their determination to do what they saw as their patriotic duty, those men denied their families the military pay allotments and allowances for which they would otherwise have been eligible. The war years were extremely hard for such families.

The recruiting campaign of the summer of 1914 was only a few weeks old when a senior Canadian military officer declared, "If Canada is to maintain her independence, the Canadian soldier must do his duty and his wife should not restrain him from selfish motives." The requirement of a wife's consent was abolished in August 1915. Men like Guelph's George Ryder enlisted first, and then told their wives.

The social pressure on women to get the men in their lives into uniforms was almost as great as that on the men themselves to enlist. Newspaper editorials told young women not to keep company with "slackers," and advised all women that "the khaki colour suits every man's complexion, unless he is yellow [implying cowardice]." Wives, sisters and sweethearts were urged to encourage — *shame* if necessary — their husbands, brothers and boyfriends to enlist. In Guelph, a recruiter made an appeal to "whole-souled women" to place no obstacles in the way of "sons, lovers and sweethearts" that might stop them from enlisting.

Many women, swept up in the tide of patriotic fervour, took things a step further. They mailed admonishing letters to young men they knew who hadn't signed up. Neatly folded inside the letters were white feathers, the mark of cowardice. Some would even patrol the streets in groups, watching for healthy-looking youths dressed in civilian clothes, and handing them white feathers. This caused undue embarrassment to men who had actually tried to enlist, but had been turned down because they didn't meet the military's physical requirements. A few men responded to the white feather by asking the women presenting it to them if they were aware that the Canadian Army Medical Corps was looking for women to volunteer as nursing sisters.

For mothers with sons of military age — or near it — the dilemma the war brought into their homes was heart-wrenching. At the start of the war, the legal age at which a youth could enlist of his own accord was eighteen (later changed to nineteen). But a boy as young as sixteen could sign up with parental permission. This was yet another spark for family turmoil. Generally, a father was more likely than a mother to be willing to give consent; not because he loved his son any less, but because he sympathized with the boy's desire to do what was "manly" in a time of national need. However, if the mother saw things differently, the result could be a divided household. Many underage youths simply ran away from home and lied about their age at the recruiting station. With the need so great to get as many bodies as possible into uniform, plenty of recruiting officers were willing to wink when a downy-faced boy swore he was eighteen. Although thousands of underage boys who had enlisted were found out and sent home, in many other instances mothers who learned of their young sons' deceptions tried to have the enlistments nullified, but were bitterly disappointed to be told that an oath to serve the king had been freely signed and could not be broken.

Even when a son's age wasn't a technical factor, his mother could have tremendous influence on his decision to enlist — or not. She might play the part of the Spartan mother who sent her soldier son off to war with instructions to come home with his shield or on it. Or she might plead that her son's real duty was to his home and family. This might especially be true in the case of a younger son who already had one or more brothers fighting — or perhaps even dead. The war sorely tested the bonds between mothers and sons, because few young men wanted to take their leave of the family home for an uncertain future without their mothers' blessings. Of the hundreds of Guelphites who filled out attestation papers, the greatest number by far named their mother as next-of-kin.

The Canadian government certainly wanted Canada's mothers to follow the Spartan example, and stepped up the rhetoric in recruiting campaigns after military officers complained that pacifist women wielded too much influence over their loved ones. One of the most dramatic newspaper ads was aimed directly at mothers who had sons of military age.

"Have You Mothered a Man?" cried the full-page spread. "Some Women Have Given Many Sons to the Country's

Cause. Some Women (Who Can) Have Not Given One."

Added to this was the rhetoric of military officers who declared that the mothers of soldiers who fell in battle should be proud to have given birth to such sons. Better to be the patriotic mother of a slain hero than the selfish mother of a cowardly slacker.

Alice Worton, a British immigrant, had six sons. Two were living in Guelph at the start of the war, and the others were in England and Western Canada. All six went to war, and they all came home. Less fortunate were Guelph mothers like Elizabeth Leslie, Agnes Russell and Elizabeth Grant, each of whom lost two sons.

Like their sisters across Canada, many Guelph women joined the labour force — some for the first time. It was an era in which the belief still prevailed — at least for the upper and middle classes — that a woman's place was in the home. Women of low-income households had long been employed as waitresses, cooks and laundresses; or were "in service" as maids and housekeepers. Women and girls from working-class families were also employed as telephone operators (a mentally and physically demanding job), and performed a wide range of hard, mind-numbing and often dangerous tasks in the textile industry, one of Guelph's largest employers.

With such a large part of the male labour force drawn off to military service, women had to fill the void. Middle-class women whose husbands were overseas became their families' principal breadwinners. There was a strong undercurrent of doubt that women could competently do "men's work." Paradoxically, there was a nagging worry that, once hired, women would expect that, after the war was over, they could keep jobs needed by returned soldiers.

The first jobs opened to women were positions as clerks and cashiers in banks and the shipping departments of express offices. Hundreds of young employees like John Martin and Arthur McKay of the Guelph branch of the Bank of Nova Scotia had set aside their pens for rifles. Bank managers were initially reluctant to hire women. They thought females were temperamentally unsuited to employment as important as banking, and would be unable to cope with the noon-hour rush that was a regular part of almost every bank's day. After women had been on the job for months and had proven they were as competent as males, managers complained that female employees required too many "breaks."

Nonetheless, the demand for women workers increased. Railroad companies accepted women into their training centres to learn to be dispatchers. At switchboards connected to model railways laid out on tables, and complete with miniature switches, signals and semaphores, female trainees were taught the complexities of running a railyard and preventing accidents on long stretches of track between communities.

Filling government contracts for war work meant that factories had to be kept humming at all hours. Although some manufacturers initially held back on hiring women, the need for workers to fill round-the-clock shifts made it inevitable that they would help shoulder the industrial workload. That women were paid less than men increased profit margins. At plants like Guelph Worsted Spinning Mills and Guelph Carpet Mills, women made military clothing and related items. At the Taylor-Forbes factory, which in peacetime manufactured domestic machinery such as lawn mowers, women engaged in the dangerous work of making munitions.

The very idea of women working night shifts in factories was radical. It went against the grain of what was considered proper, and posed the possibility of scandals. As a safeguard, the Young Women's Christian Association was engaged to supervise female workers. Colonel E.J. Chambers, the Chief Press Censor for the federal government, requested that newspaper editors "exclude from publication" any reports of women being molested going to and from their places of employment, because such reports might discourage the use of female labour on night shifts in munitions factories.

In some of Canada's larger urban centres, women formed rifle clubs and organized home guard groups with the idea that they might serve as an auxiliary to the local militia, doing guard duty and other tasks related to national security. But the press made light of their effort and even denounced it as deviant, so it wasn't followed up to any significant degree in smaller communities like Guelph. Instead, Guelph women became active in organizations like the Imperial Order of the Daughters of the Empire and the Women's Institute.

Supported by the newspaper through free publicity, the women of the IODE and the WI raised money for the Red Cross, the Belgian Relief Fund and other war-related charities. They hosted public-speaking events at which the guests of honour were politicians, military leaders and returned soldiers, whose speeches usually focused on the need for every man to do his duty.

The women's groups got together to roll bandages and knit socks. To promote patriotism in the young, they held essay-writing contests in public schools. The students competed for prizes by writing on such topics as "Why

Canada Is at War" and "Why Germany Is a Threat to Christian Civilization." The women pressed school boards to have patriotism taught as a subject.

Among the most pragmatic activities was the promotion of household management that voluntarily conformed with wartime food-control regulations. Located in the middle of agriculturally rich southern Ontario, Guelph had never experienced food shortages. Its markets had always brimmed with the bounty from the surrounding farm and pasture country. An efficient transportation system kept grocery store shelves stocked with relatively inexpensive imported "staples" like sugar, tea and coffee. But war meant shortages of foodstuffs, not only because sea lanes had become dangerous for shipping, but also because much of the nation's agricultural production was being shipped overseas to feed the Allied armies and millions of civilians who would otherwise starve.

"Household management" for many families was in women's hands. Mothers had to adjust to a situation in which certain commodities were suddenly very expensive or not available at all. Molasses was a cheap substitute for other sweeteners. Tea leaves could be used more than once. Meat didn't have to be served for supper every day. Backyards could be turned into vegetable gardens.

The paper regularly published "War Menus" issued by the Office of the Food Controller for Canada. Readers were assured that they were prepared by "Domestic Science Experts." By following the menus regularly, women would "Save Wheat, Beef and Bacon for the men at the front," and still provide their families with nourishing meals. The War Menu for a Friday in January, 1918 was:

Breakfast
Cornmeal porridge, toast, parsley omelette,
tea or coffee

Dinner [lunch]
Fried cod, tomatoes, potatoes, fruit tart

Supper
Cheese relish on toast, emergency biscuits,
plum preserve, war cake, tea

The War Menus included recipes for such items as emergency biscuits (also called drop biscuits), cheese relish, war bread, war cake and Oriental stew (which had nothing Oriental about it). Basic ingredients included such items as stale bread crumbs, brown sugar, salt, raisins and lard, with a little curry powder, cayenne pepper or cinnamon for flavour. Cornmeal and potato flour replaced white wheat flour, and mutton was the main substitute for beef and pork. The Office of the Food Controller urged women to have their families participate in "Fish Fridays," a practice already followed by Roman Catholics.

An ad titled "A Woman's Way" said that while a woman couldn't shoulder a rifle, she could help win the war by buying Canadian-made goods instead of imports. "Say 'Made in Canada' Every Time You Make a Purchase" the ad concluded. This recognition of women's economic power was indicative of their emergence as a force that could no longer be ignored. The suffragist movement had long been fighting for women's political rights. Although the war had somewhat disrupted progress, because of the association of some leading suffragists with socialism and pacifism, by the summer of 1917 women had won the right to vote in provincial elections in the Western provinces and Ontario.

Robert Borden's government expressed its wish to acknowledge women's contribution to the war effort by extending the voting franchise at the federal level. Borden saw women as a vital voting block that would support conscription. In 1917, the controversial *Military Voters Act* and *Wartime Elections Act* extended the federal vote to nursing sisters in the Canadian Army Medical Corps and to close female relatives of men serving in the armed forces. Soldier's Wife and Grit Callander's mother, and all the other wives and mothers of Guelph men serving in the CEF, could now mark ballots in federal elections.

However, many women's suffragists denounced the acts as discriminatory half-measures. The *Wartime Elections Act* also disenfranchised conscientious objectors and thousands of immigrants from Germany and from nations that were Germany's allies. Loyal immigrants in working-class neighbourhoods like Guelph's Ward, who had supported causes like the Patriotic Fund and the Belgian Relief Fund, lost a fundamental democratic right of Canadian citizenship.

After winning the election of December 17 and then seeing his much-contested conscription bill passed in parliament, Borden declared that extending the franchise to all eligible women would have a positive influence on public life. On May 24, 1918, the extension became law. All female Canadian citizens over the age of twenty-one — with the exception of those excluded by racial restrictions aimed at the Asian minority — could vote in federal elections. To Guelphites strolling down Wyndham Street that afternoon, the world would have appeared just as it had the day before. But the change was monumental.

Salvation Army knitters in Guelph. Canadian soldiers wrote home requesting clothing of every sort, but socks were in the greatest demand. (Courtesy of Guelph Museums 1985.31.2)

CHAPTER 14
SOCKS AND MACHINE GUNS

On November 25, 1915, shortly after a report announcing that John Alfred "Fred" Laurie had been killed in action, the following notice appeared on the front page of the paper:

> A friend of his writes a rather pathetic little letter to the Mercury, stating that she had prepared a box to send him for Christmas, but now he is gone, she wishes the name of some boy at the front to whom such a gift would be acceptable. Some readers might send a name to this paper, and it will be published for the benefit of our thoughtful and kind hearted correspondent.

The unidentified correspondent's act of kindness was just one small example of the support for the men at the front that was in evidence all over Canada. Sending comfort parcels to soldiers was one of the most important ways people at home could participate in the war effort. The parcels were vital to the morale of the troops, and they provided every man, woman and child in the community with an opportunity to "do their bit."

Of course, Christmas was when young men who had never been away from their families before felt homesickness most acutely. But, in the trenches, there was no day a parcel from home — even from a kind-hearted stranger — wasn't welcome.

Families packed boxes with anything they thought would make life at the front more endurable. Cigarettes and other tobacco products were regarded as necessities, and topped the list. Food was a close second.

In spite of government censorship, it was well known that the soldiers lived on a dreary diet of bread, oatmeal, "bully beef" and whatever the cooks could boil in a pot. To break the monotony, families sent cookies, biscuits, candies, chocolate, cheese, jam, tea and Ovaltine. Those gifts were like exotic fare to the men in the trenches. The recipient of such a parcel almost invariably shared the contents with his mates.

The Canadians hadn't been in the trenches very long before families began to receive letters requesting basic personal hygiene items: soap, combs, handkerchiefs, toothbrushes and tooth powder, shaving soap and brushes, and razors. Ads requested men to donate razors.

During their first winter in the trenches, the Canadians found that their army-issue clothing was inadequate protection from the damp chill of Western Europe — so different from the winter weather they'd known at home. In their letters they asked for mittens, scarves and sweaters. Guelph merchants did a thriving trade as soldiers' families bought up those items. They also sold a lot of yarn, because much of the warm clothing destined for the front was made in homes.

Mothers and wives, sisters and sweethearts, spent hours knitting comfort items not only for their own men, but also for the rest of the soldiers. The local paper called on the women of Guelph to form knitting groups and donate their work to the cause of the Empire. Not all of a soldier's clothing needs could easily be filled by a pair of knitting needles. Private John McTague, a former employee of the *Mercury*, wrote to his sister, "I would be very grateful if you would send underwear to me . . . We get a clean suit about once a week, but [it] has generally been inhabited before and so is not altogether comfortable."

Perhaps no other article of clothing was in greater demand by the Canadians in the trenches than socks. Large sections of the Western Front were quagmires of mud. The trenches were hardly ever dry, so soldiers' feet were almost always wet. In cold weather their feet froze. Many of the men suffered from an extremely painful affliction called trench foot. The situation became part of a national scandal.

Contracts for boots, uniforms and other military needs went to industrialists who had connections in high places, including people as influential as Sir Sam Hughes. To maximize profits from the lucrative government contracts, manufacturers produced their merchandise as cheaply as possible. As a result, Canadian soldiers were clothed in uniforms that fell apart in the dank conditions of the trenches. The shoddy boots drew the most complaints.

While the newspapers reported that the men defending civilization and the Empire were slogging through knee-deep mud in boots that might as well have been made of paper, soldiers were writing letters home pleading for socks. Knitting alone at home, or with groups in church halls and community centres, women worked their fingers to the bone making thousands of pairs of socks. They filled a need and they gained no profit. They were motivated by love and duty.

The men were grateful. On January 15, 1916, under the heading "Thanks From The Trenches," the paper published some of the numerous letters soldiers had written to Mrs. B.F. Petrie, President of the Guelph Garrison Ladies' Club, whose socks had arrived in time to be distributed among the various units at Christmas. One of the letters was written by Lieutenant Benjamin B. McConkey, an artillery officer from Guelph:

> I am writing to thank you on behalf of my men for the twenty-five pairs of socks which arrived this morning. I only wish that you will know how we all appreciate the kindness of the ladies at home and the good work you are doing. I am giving the socks to the men tomorrow, Christmas Day. They could not have arrived at a more appropriate time.

Another item eagerly received by Guelph boys in the trenches was the local newspaper itself. A copy of the hometown newspaper, even though weeks old, was a special physical and emotional connection to a life before the madness of the war. In the lulls between battles, a Guelph man could sit in his dugout, his feet warmed by a new pair of socks and eat a cookie or smoke a cigarette from his parcel while he perused the news from home. He certainly wanted to know what the papers in Canada were saying about the war, but reports on the ordinary events in his own community helped him maintain his sense of belonging. What teams were leading in the school hockey and baseball leagues? Who had got married, had a baby, died — or joined the ranks of the enlisted. One Guelph soldier told his family that he read every page of the newspapers they sent him, even the advertisements.

While the people of Guelph were busy filling "comfort packages," they were also being called upon for financial support. "Fight or Pay" was the slogan. The cost of the war was enormous. The federal government was selling war bonds, but was also already considering imposing a "war tax" on income. It was a very unpopular measure, and would still be insufficient to make up for the growing drain on the economy. People were suspicious of the tax because they believed much of the money would be squandered through government inefficiency or land in the pockets of profiteers.

One way to encourage people to open their wallets was to organize fundraisers for the purchase of specific items needed at the front. Contributors would see themselves as having some control over where their money went, and their names would be published in the newspaper. People were asked to contribute to such special subscriptions as the Motor Ambulance Fund.

When the newspaper reported that a Guelph physician, Dr. Henry Howitt, had sent the Militia Department a cheque for $1,000 to be used for the purchase of a machine

184 Wartime: The First World War in a Canadian Town

gun, other donors quickly followed suit. MPP Samuel Carter told the paper by phone, "I read the *Mercury* last night about what Guelph was doing to provide machine guns, and while I believe the government should furnish them, this is not the time to stand on ceremonies. I have no boys to go, and I cannot go myself, but you can state that my family is willing to put up the price for one machine gun. This war has to be won, and people must make sacrifices to do it. I hope there will be many of them given by the people of Guelph."

After the newspaper printed Carter's statement, the faculty at the Ontario Agricultural College contributed enough money to pay for three machine guns. One hundred school inspectors from across Ontario who were at the OAC for a two-week course chipped in enough cash for one more. Clarks' Rifles, a local militia unit, announced their intention to collect enough money from members for yet another machine gun. Such fundraisers became the focus of civic pride, with communities vying to outdo each other.

With so much of the country's agricultural and industrial production being diverted from domestic needs to the war effort, there were shortages of almost everything. As ingredients for making pies and cakes became scarce, a country pastry with a filling made from brown sugar gained popularity. For the first time, urban Canadians began to enjoy butter tarts.

As the rationing of white flour became ever more stringent, housewives had to feed their families bread made from such ingredients as potato flour, oats and barley. The newspapers called it "Victory Bread." The people who had to eat it called it "war bread."

Besides being asked to help bear the staggering financial burden of waging war, Guelphites were constantly reminded of the conflict's tragic human cost. One could hardly open the paper without seeing ads crying out for assistance for the war's victims. The ads were designed to appeal to the public's patriotism, Christianity and fundamental human empathy.

In a poster-sized ad illustrated with the image of an army medic assisting a wounded soldier while the spirit of Christ, "the Great Volunteer in mankind's service" looks on, the British Red Cross called on Canadians to "Give and Heal . . . Your gift may save some hero's life."

Ads for the Belgian Relief Fund, an international organization chaired by future American president Herbert Hoover, pleaded for money to help the desperate people of "Little Belgium." One ad carried an illustration of little boys, looking like so many Oliver Twists, holding empty plates. "We must not let these Belgian children starve," it said. "$2.50 Feeds A Belgian Family One Month."

The Wellington County branch of the Ontario Children's Aid Society, headquartered in Guelph, announced a plan to bring eight orphaned Belgian children to the city and place them in the Children's Shelter on Clark Street until homes could be found for them. Requests went out through the newspaper and the churches for money, food, clothing and other essentials. Many Guelphites responded, but a reporter who visited the shelter was disappointed with some of the donations.

"There's a lot of stuff sent to the shelter that might be better thrown at the heads of the donors," he wrote. "Some of it is so much cast-off as to be fit for the rag bag."

The steady stream of cash donations to the Belgian Relief Fund evidently caught the attention of unethical opportunists who sought to capitalize on the public's generosity toward the victims of war. The Belgians weren't the only people suffering atrocities. In the eastern theatre of the war, the government of Turkey, which was allied with Germany, was engaged in a campaign of genocide against the people of Armenia. Simon Solman, an Armenian immigrant living in Guelph, asked the paper to warn citizens about fraudsters collecting for an Armenian Relief Fund. He said local Armenians were contributing to a central fund in the United States, and had not sent out collectors in Guelph. Anyone claiming to represent an Armenian Relief Fund should be reported to the police.

The Canadian Patriotic Fund (CPF), however, was legitimate. It was established in August 1914 through the efforts of Montreal businessman, politician and philanthropist Sir Herbert B. Ames. Though the Governor General of Canada was a patron, and the federal minister of finance served as treasurer, it was a private organization. Its purpose was to raise money for the relief of families who were in financial need because fathers and husbands were fighting at the front or had become casualties. Although that initially meant British families, because the CEF wouldn't reach the front until the spring of 1915, the CPF assured married Canadian enlisted men that their families would be cared for in their absence.

On September 23, 1914, the local paper published a full-page CPF ad graced with photographs of King George V and Queen Mary, and an illustration of the Union Jack crossed with the Canadian Red Ensign. Along with the words "GIVE! GIVE! GIVE! GIVE!" were two lines from Rudyard Kipling's "Recessional," a poem with which most Guelphites would have been familiar:

> Lord God of Hosts be with us yet,
> Lest we forget, Lest we forget.

The ad was a "Call to Guelph in the name of Women and Children," and asked citizens what share of the burden they would take to help save the Empire and the freedom and happiness of its peoples. "Everybody will be called upon to contribute. The widow's mite will be just as acceptable as the hundreds of the well-to-do."

The following evening, the Guelph Veterans' Association, local militia regiments and the Salvation Army band paraded through downtown. A "Monster Mass Meeting" was held in front of City Hall to promote the Patriotic Fund. Admission was free, ladies were welcome and all were invited to join in the singing of "It's a Long Way to Tipperary" and, of course, "God Save the King." Teams of collectors were organized to canvas every neighbourhood in the city.

On September 28, the team leaders met for a luncheon at the Kandy Kitchen to turn in their donations. The paper reported that the people of Guelph were "Putting Patriotism in Concrete Form," and had met the first goal of $15,000. Some collectors had stationed themselves at factory doors where men arriving for work were asked to donate a day's pay. No one refused. The employers also made generous donations. The Taylor-Forbes, James Goldie and Page-Hersey companies were among those that wrote cheques for $500.

In residential areas, people gave what they could, even if it was just nickels and dimes. Some who had no cash on hand donated jewellery and keepsakes to be sold for the benefit of the fund. One collector told of a woman who stood at her door and tearfully said that never in her life had she so wanted to give to a cause, but there was no money in the house and none coming in. She and a few others like her could only express their sympathy for "the cause."

Donations came from the guards and staff at the Ontario Reformatory, the Imperial Order of the Daughters of the Empire and the Masonic Lodge. Guelph City Council contributed $2,000. The paper said Guelph was making the kind of sacrifices that count.

In January 1916, the Patriotic Fund launched another drive in Guelph, with a goal of $60,000. By that time the CEF had been in the thick of the fighting for months, and the casualty list had grown longer than anybody had imagined it would a year earlier. The families of 181 Guelph soldiers, about 750 people, were receiving Patriotic Fund assistance, with the number expected to climb.

In order to receive financial support, families had to accept visits from CPF investigators who determined eligibility and level of need. The investigators, usually women, were also volunteer social workers who advised families on such matters as budgeting, nutrition, sanitation, personal hygiene and child care. They were also advocates of conservative views on entitlement and moral values. They could, without any provision for appeal, disqualify families they considered undeserving. The needy families of slain and wounded soldiers resented what they considered a condescending intrusion into their personal lives.

Months of contributing money to war-related causes, and donating everything from socks to machine guns, hadn't made Guelphites stingy. But people were starting to ask questions about responsibility for the care and support of soldiers' families in need. That was the main issue when Sir Herbert Ames walked onto the stage of the Guelph Opera House on January 14. Raising money had become increasingly difficult, so Ames had been making personal appearances in communities like Guelph to explain the workings of the Patriotic Fund and urge people to continue giving.

"It is the duty of those left behind to take care of the families of those who are doing their bit . . . We [the CPF] have one common aim, we have one flag, one fund, and one purse, and all who can should put into that purse."

Ames said that people were presenting his volunteer collectors with what he considered "excuses" not to contribute. The one most commonly heard was that there should be no need for a Patriotic Fund in the first place, because the federal government should take care of the soldiers' families. Ames pointed out that the government paid a "separation allowance" of $20 a month to the wife of every married enlisted man. But in many cases that was not enough. A mother with five children to feed and clothe had a much harder time than a mother with just one or two children. In that mother's situation, Ames said, the Patriotic Fund "came to the rescue."

Ames said some people complained that soldiers' wives received too much money and used it to buy "things they were never able to purchase before." His response to that "excuse" was, "Even if it is so, who has a better right to do so than the dependant of the man who is serving his king and country and risking his life to do so?"

In the days following Ames's stopover in Guelph, the local Patriotic Fund Committee again made the Kandy Kitchen its headquarters. A "thermometer" out front marked the rise of donations toward $60,000. Guelph City Council pledged a civic grant of $24,000 to be paid at a rate of $2,000 a month, based on the promised support of what was reported as "a number of big men in Guelph who will get behind these schemes and see them through."

However, it seemed that not all of Guelph's "big men" were cooperative. Charles L. Dunbar, local secretary for the CPF, said that one affluent citizen "would not contribute to the cause because his money was tied up in stocks and bonds." The newspaper posed the question, "Does that afford any reason why the rest of us should not do our own duty?"

Another ad asked Guelphites to consider what their city would look like after a Zeppelin bombing raid. "Because we are by good fortune not actually in it, we are, nevertheless, of it. To all of us is not given the privilege of wearing the Khaki, but the responsibility is the same to us all."

To strike a sentimental nerve, the newspaper published "To Those They Left Behind," composed by Irish Canadian poet Michael A. Hargadon of Montreal for the Patriotic Fund. Each of the first five stanzas deals with specific loved ones in soldiers' families: wives, children, mothers, fathers and old folks.

> You still possess a mother
> To give her love to you;
> The boys who went have mothers
> Who dearly love them too;
> Then for the fond old mothers
> Who watch and fret and pray
> Arise above all selfishness
> And give your mite today.

The last stanzas press home the importance of donating.

> Thus giving and thus helping
> You will be aiding on
> The struggle that will have no end
> Till victory has shone;
> Each bill you give is as a shell
> Shot at the Kaiser's heart;
>
> Shoot, shoot and shoot until that hell
> Is shot and rent apart.

Once again, the CPF drive was successful. The thermometer in front of the Kandy Kitchen hit $60,000. But questions still lingered as to whether the government should take greater responsibility for the care of soldiers' families, or leave them to the whims and stigma of charity.

Guelph Chief of Police Frederick Randall enforced such extraordinary wartime measures as the confiscation of wireless sets, but had to temper compliance with regulations with compassion in the matter of "foreigners" in his community. (Courtesy of Guelph Museums 2009.32.2436)

CHAPTER 15
SPIES AND SABOTEURS

Stunning news swept through Guelph on March 6, 1916. The local paper reported that Charles Respa, a suspected German agent, had been secretly held in the Wellington County jail. By the time Guelphites read the story, Respa had gained international notoriety.

Respa was a German who had immigrated to the United States in 1904. Aside from a brief period in 1912 when he tried homesteading in Alberta, he had lived and worked in Detroit. In 1915, Respa was one of several men recruited as spies and saboteurs by German agents in the still neutral United States. He felt that his first duty was to the Fatherland.

After he had gone on a reconnaissance mission to Winnipeg to gather information on railway lines, Respa and several confederates were ordered to help disrupt the Canadian war effort and spread fear through bombing attacks. On the night of June 21, 1915, they crossed the Detroit River and placed time-bombs against the walls of the Windsor Armoury and Walkerville's Peabody Textile mill, which made military clothing. The bomb at the Armoury failed to explode and was discovered by a sentry. There was a blast at the Peabody factory, but damage was minimal and nobody was hurt.

Within days, Windsor police found stashes of dynamite near several munitions and automotive factories in Windsor. Detroit police and the American Secret Service rounded up German suspects. One of them informed on Respa. He was arrested by the Ontario Provincial Police on August 29 while attending a picnic on Bois Blanc (Boblo) Island.

Respa was initially locked up in the Essex County jail in Sandwich. However, there were reports of suspicious-looking people in the town. From across the river came rumours of German sympathizers holding clandestine meetings and taking up collections of funds for his "liberation." Suspecting a plot to break Respa out of jail and smuggle him across the border, Canadian authorities quietly moved him to Guelph. He remained there even during the preliminary court proceedings that began in Sandwich on February 8, 1916, in which his co-conspirators were questioned.

In the meantime, Respa's name was in newspaper head-lines across Canada and the United States. The planting of the bomb at the Windsor Armoury was condemned in the press as a particularly heinous act. If it had detonated, scores of sleeping soldiers could have been killed or maimed.

On the day Guelphites were informed that Respa had been a prisoner in their local jail, he was already back in Sandwich to stand trial on charges of espionage and sabotage in time of war. With the exception of the jail's guards, no one in the city had laid eyes on the notorious enemy agent. But the paper published a detailed account of his trial. Respa was convicted and sentenced to life imprisonment in the Kingston Penitentiary. He would be deported to Germany in 1924.

The fact that a German agent had been held in a Guelph jail cell brought home the threat of "the enemy in our midst." Within a week of Respa's conviction, a man named William Colombo was arrested by Guelph police and fined $19 after an altercation in a livery stable during which he'd made anti-British and pro-German remarks. He'd allegedly said, "I would like to walk knee-deep in British blood, and shake hands with the Kaiser."

Fear of "enemy aliens" actually went back even to August 1914, when the federal government brought the *War Measures Act* into force, suspending or limiting the civil rights of "foreigners" and making them liable for arrest on the slightest suspicion. Guelph had a large immigrant population, with many of the people concentrated in the Ward. Aside from the Italians, who made up the largest ethnic group, there were a few Germans and a mixture of Austrians, Hungarians, Ukrainians and Poles, who were generally lumped together in the catch-all term "Austrians." There was a large ethnic German population in nearby Berlin. North of Berlin the countryside was populated by German-speaking Mennonite farmers whose antiquated lifestyle had always caused them to be regarded as outsiders.

Before August 1914 had passed, newspapers had reported alleged enemy activity in other Ontario communities. Two unidentified men started a fire at the Wolseley Barracks in London late one night, and shot at a sentry, wounding him in the hand. The fire was extinguished before it could cause much damage. Then a signalman was attacked by five men on a section of the Northwestern Railway near London. They stabbed him — though not fatally — and escaped after destroying a signal box, apparently in hope of causing a train wreck. "They were undoubtedly German agents," the Toronto *Globe* said.

At Fort William (part of present-day Thunder Bay), a sentry surprised a group of men wrecking equipment at the government wireless station under cover of darkness. They opened fire and wounded him as they fled. The same saboteurs were believed to be responsible for an attempt on the wireless station at Sault Ste. Marie. They fled into the woods when a sentry discovered them "prowling around" and fired four warning shots. Newspaper editorials expressed concern about "trigger happy" sentries posing a danger to the public. The Ministry of Militia and Defence responded:

> The order as sent out today to militiamen employed in protection of public buildings, works, etc., is explicit. It is that they shall not hesitate to take effective measures to prevent the perpetration of malicious injury, and should sentries, pickets or patrols be obliged to use weapons and open fire, their aim shall be directed at and not over the heads of offenders. Local papers have been asked to publish warnings that sentries in such cases are to "shoot to kill."

On December 1, 1914, the newspapers reported the discovery of a nefarious German plan for the invasion of Canada. German sympathizers in the United States, coming from as far away as New Orleans, would enter Canada by train, posing as pilgrims heading for the shrine of Sainte-Anne-de-Beaupré in Quebec. Among them would be soldiers from the Kaiser's army. Arms would be waiting for them. When their number eventually built up to five or six thousand, they would make a surprise attack on Quebec City, seizing munitions factories and capturing the big guns that guarded the St. Lawrence River. The historic gateway to Canada would then be open to a general invasion.

"Fortunately, their plans have come to nought," said the newspaper, "as the British fleet still holds the supremacy of the seas."

Early in 1915, Guelphites were reminded that the enemy could be anywhere when Toronto merchant Emil Nerlich and his wife Hedwig were arrested on charges of treason. The German-born couple had been in Canada for twenty-seven years, and Emil was well-respected in Toronto's business community. They were accused of trading with the enemy and helping a former German military officer named Arthur Zirzow escape from Canada so he could join the Kaiser's army. The charges against Hedwig were eventually dropped, and Emil was convicted on a lesser charge of conspiring to commit an indictable offence.

The Nerlich case was still in the papers when on February 3, 1916, disaster struck in Ottawa. A horrific fire engulfed the Centre Block of the Parliament Building. Seven people were killed. Prime Minister Borden himself was fortunate to escape unharmed. Although an investigation would eventually conclude that the cause of fire had been accidental, in the immediate aftermath the outraged people of Canada had no doubt that German agents had struck at the very heart of Canadian democracy. If the Kaiser's saboteurs could find their way into what was supposed to be the most well-guarded building in the country, no place was safe from attack.

Not even the Boy Scouts were immune to the threat of enemy infiltration. Well-organized along British cadet lines, holding a great measure of public trust, and sworn to do their duty to God and the king, the Scouts were regarded as the army's eager young helpers. They therefore had access to military camps and other places closed to the public. Like just about every other Canadian city or town, Guelph had a Boy Scout troop. In October 1914, the *Globe* reported that German spies had been disguising themselves as Scoutmasters and even Boy Scouts in order to gain entry to prohibited places. One, characterized as a "dangerous international spy," supposedly plied sentries with liquor in the hope that they would divulge secret information or allow him to enter posted areas. This man had allegedly been seen in London. People in surrounding cities like Guelph kept a wary eye for bogus Boy Scouts.

Two Guelph men who belonged to the International Bible Students Association were arrested for possession of literature considered to be subversive: *The Finished Mystery* and *Studies of Scripture*. Both had been banned under the *War Measures Act*. *Studies of Scripture* contained controversial views on Christianity, and *The Finished Mystery* had passages considered derogatory to Britain and her role in the war. The two Bible students could have faced penalties of five years in prison and a $5,000 fine. However, the magistrate let them off with fines of $100 each and a stern warning.

Guelph experienced a sabotage scare when the city's drinking water was found to be contaminated. Police were told of suspicious-looking characters loitering around a location in the Ward where the pipeline that carried water from springs in the Arkell Hills to the south were covered by just a few inches of dirt. An examination of the entire pipeline right to the water's source by scientists and engineers from Toronto concluded that the saboteurs were cattle, whose waste was seeping into the pipe through cracks in a section shallowly buried under pastureland. Wartime vigilance had proven its worth, even if it had rooted out no foreign agents.

Hundreds of Guelph men employed in factories and foundries had joined the army. Their absence from the labour force created a conundrum. Women filled some factory jobs, but they were considered unsuited for work that called for brawn and the stamina to endure long hours of hard physical labour. Male "foreigners" had been working alongside Canadian- and British-born men at such employment for years. With the coming of war, large numbers of "foreign" workers were fired because they were deemed untrustworthy. For the same reason, they were not wanted in the military. The result was a growing list of unemployed men turning to Guelph's municipal offices for relief.

Foreigners on the dole were on a type of parole, and were required to report regularly to an "enemy alien" registry office. Failure to do so meant being disqualified for assistance, and possible arrest. That placed a severe restriction on freedom to seek employment elsewhere. The Guelph newspaper reported that the city would provide such unfortunate men with enough work for them to "make a dollar or two" so they wouldn't starve. That was a stop-gap measure that didn't meet the needs of the men and their families.

The city faced sharp criticism for hiring foreign workers. Some native-born Canadians didn't want to work alongside "the enemy." There were protests that "Austrians" were taking jobs away from "Englishmen." The city cut back on relief work, forcing desperate men to take the risk of skipping parole to hunt for work in other communities. Transient men wound up homeless on unfamiliar streets. They were not regarded simply as tramps, but as potential enemy agents. A series of incidents that occurred in Guelph typified the situation across the country.

A Hungarian immigrant from Toronto went into Guelph's police court seeking a meal and shelter. Chief Randall questioned him through an interpreter. The man said he had lived and worked in Guelph previously, and had returned hoping to find a job. Randall was satisfied that he posed no threat, and allowed him to go on his way.

Many people in town felt that Randall should have taken a tougher line. There was growing animosity against "enemy aliens" begging for food and shelter at city hall and the police station. Municipal police officials like Randall were at a loss over what to do about unemployed "Austrians" who had committed no crimes, but were unwanted and resented.

Weeks later, in May 1915, six men whom the newspaper called "Austrians" showed up at the police court. They said they were out of work, penniless and hungry. Randall saw to it that they were fed, and then he contacted Colonel Arthur P. Sherwood, the Commissioner of the Dominion Police in Ottawa. Sherwood's instructions were that all of Guelph's "Austrians" were to be rounded up and put on a train to Toronto. From there they would be transported to a detention camp at Kapuskasing, to be "taken care of."

On the morning of Saturday, May 15, a court order was sent to "every Austrian and Hungarian in the city" instructing them to report to the police station by 11:45 a.m. Married men with families were allowed to remain in the city, but armed guards escorted more than fifty single men to the train station while a large crowd watched. According to the paper, the men seemed happy that they were going to a place where they would get regular meals. Across Canada, more than eight thousand "enemy aliens" were similarly rounded up and packed off to detention camps. The general resentment felt toward them was reflected in the statement of one reporter. "Germans know all right that they have become enemies of the British Empire, but the Austrians seem to think that they are still our friends." Meanwhile, factory owners faced a dilemma: they needed labourers, and sometimes the only men available for hire were the "Austrians," whom they didn't want.

Aside from simple bigotry, fear of sabotage was the principal reason for mistrust of foreigners in the workplace. In Guelph, that fear was borne out by a mysterious fire in Hespeler (now part of Cambridge), a few miles to the southwest. On February 5, 1916, while employees were on their lunch break, a fire broke out in the main shop of the Jardine Company, which had been manufacturing munitions. By the time firemen got the blaze under control, it had done sufficient damage to shut the plant down for several weeks. The cause of the fire was unknown, but arson was suspected. An "Austrian" calling himself John Schmidt was arrested. An investigation showed that he had worked in munitions plants in several communities, using a different name in each one. He was charged with incendiarism.

That evening, before the article about the Hespeler fire had even gone to press, wild rumours swept through Guelph. One false story had a second munitions factory set ablaze in nearby Galt. Others, equally groundless, claimed bridges at the border with the United States had been blown.

Panicky factory owners, especially those whose plants were producing war materials, were calling the police station demanding protection for their properties. The police received an anonymous tip that Guelph's Winter Fair buildings, which were being used by the militia, and the Armoury were to be targeted. Chief Randall was aware that the tip could be a hoax, but with the country still in shock after the Parliament Building fire, he couldn't afford to take chances.

Randall didn't have enough constables to cover all the

potential trouble spots, so he called the military authorities. Soldiers on leave who were among the downtown crowds were suddenly summoned to emergency duty. A few were even rousted from their seats in theatres. They were dispatched to guard several factories and the Winter Fair buildings. Extra sentries surrounded the Armoury.

The alarm spread to other Southern Ontario communities. Mayors and industrialists wired Sir Sam Hughes in Ottawa, demanding military protection. The Ontario Provincial Police in Wingham arrested a German immigrant named Adolphe Schatte, who was the local bandmaster, on a charge of possessing explosives. He was released on parole and forbidden to leave town. Soldiers in St. Catharines and London were placed on guard at munitions factories. In Brantford, Member of Parliament W.F. Cockshutt renewed the call for the internment of every enemy alien and the protection of every public building and munitions factory. "If there are any vipers in our midst, they must be exterminated," he said in a speech before his riding's Liberal Club. "This war will not be won by gentle means."

Over the next week, the Guelph Fire Department was called upon several times to extinguish blazes in various parts of the city, including one that gutted an automotive repair shop. None of those fires involved strategic public buildings or factories doing war work, and all of them proved to be accidental. But the unusual frequency of the outbreaks had the city on edge, and not everyone was convinced that they weren't deliberately set.

Before the war's end, there would be further local stories about suspected enemy activities. One came in November 1916, when an inspector at a munitions plant in Hamilton discovered about forty shells that had been "plugged," which meant they could explode prematurely. Two employees, Eric N. Nylin and his son Eric H. Nylin, were arrested. They claimed to be Serbians, but were found actually to be German Swedes. When their lawyer requested bail, the magistrate refused. He told the prisoners, "It will be safer in jail for you than outside when the people learn the facts." Two months later the pair was released, because of insufficient evidence.

Rail was the principal means of inter-city travel at that time, so, like other Canadians, Guelphites would have been horrified to learn of the June 30, 1917, derailment of the CNR Ottawa to Toronto train near the town of Thurlow (now part of Belleville). The engine and all of the cars left the track and ploughed into a swamp. Miraculously, none of the passengers, whose number included MPs and military officers, suffered serious injury. The subsequent investigation turned up conclusive evidence that a switch had been sabotaged. "A Diabolical Plot" said the Guelph newspaper.

A few weeks later, a German immigrant named Franz Moran was arrested by Guelph police on a charge of sending money to Germany through friends in Switzerland. The newspaper called him "A real Hapsburger," and lamented the fact that hundreds of dollars of "good Canadian earned money" had found its way to Germany. Moran confessed, and was sent to Kapuskasing.

However, despite all the reports of conspiracies and plots that punctuated the wartime atmosphere of fear and suspicion, the closest Guelphites ever really came to an actual German agent was when Charles Respa was secretly lodged in their county jail. And the only "enemy aliens" they would set eyes on were a few dozen unemployed, hungry, bewildered "Austrians" under armed escort, boarding a train that would take them to a detention camp.

Delivery wagons load up at a Guelph coal yard. Wartime shortages of such vital commodities as fuel struck every community in Canada, and were sometimes exacerbated by corruption and favouritism. (Courtesy of Guelph Museums 1994.53.2)

CHAPTER 16
SHORTAGES AND THE BATTLE OF GUELPH

In December 1917, a housewife wrote a letter to the editor in which she complained of being victimized since her husband had gone overseas. As she put it, "Some of us soldier dependents are left to our fates." She said that before he went off to war, her husband had received their landlord's promise that the rent for their house would remain the same. Then, when the man of the house was gone, the landlord raised the rent by two dollars a month. She said he did not raise her next door neighbour's rent.

Even more exasperating was the matter of coal. The housewife said her husband had paid the coal dealer in advance, and had trusted him to be as good as his word and make deliveries. But when her coal bin ran low, he put her off repeatedly with the excuse that the coal supply in the city was short. And yet, she said, she knew of other homes, more affluent than hers, that had two furnaces as well as fireplaces in some of the rooms, that were getting deliveries from the same dealer.

It galled the housewife that women from those privileged homes were among the many people who came to her door seeking donations to various war-related causes, when she couldn't even get desperately needed coal that had already been paid for. But her principal complaint was against the businessmen who took advantage of a woman who was on her own:

> Now what would you think my husband and brothers would feel like if they knew how I was treated? They are sacrificing everything for such men as I speak of. Does it give us good women any courage to go on when we have to face people like this every day? . . . I would like to know how much more they require of us who have already given all we have to give. Is there no one in this Royal City of ours loyal enough to see that soldiers' dependents come first and not last?

The housewife signed the letter, "One of Hundreds."

The letter's author might very well have been taken advantage of by unscrupulous businessmen who saw a wife whose husband was absent as an easy mark for unethical business practices. And it's quite likely true that the well-off were preferred customers. Houses with two furnaces in the basement and extra fireplaces weren't generally found in working-class neighbourhoods. But the fact remained that the war brought a coal shortage to Guelph. It was a home front crisis that struck many Canadian communities.

Coal fed furnaces and big iron kitchen stoves. Few Guelph homes had the new-fangled electric "fireless cookers." The war effort was devouring coal from the mines in Nova Scotia and Western Canada, although those regions still had enough to meet their own domestic needs. But Ontario relied on supplies from the United States. The coal that was burned in factories and homes in Toronto, Hamilton, Guelph and scores of other cities and towns came by rail and Great Lakes freighters from the mines of Pennsylvania and Ohio.

But the war had also strained the Americans' ability to meet the demand, especially after the United States entered the conflict in the spring of 1917. American factories were now in operation around the clock producing war materials for their own military, as well as for the European Allies. As the demand for coal surpassed supply, the United States government adopted drastic conservation measures, which included cutting back on exports to Canada.

In almost any other year, the people of Guelph might have dealt with a coal shortage through careful rationing and a minimum of discomfort. But the winter of 1917–18 was exceptionally cold. Whole families could huddle together in bed under extra quilts for warmth at night, but what were they to do when there was no coal for the kitchen stove? Other fuel was available from farmers who owned woodlots, for those who could afford to pay for it. The bitter cold was creeping into the rooms and corridors of the Homewood Sanitarium and St. Joseph's and Guelph General hospitals because the dealers who supplied those institutions had run out. Only a loan of coal from the Canadian Pacific Railway kept the hospitals' patients from freezing. Even when a shipment of American coal reached Canada, there was no guarantee that all, if any, of it would reach communities like

Guelph. The local newspaper learned of reports that the Grand Trunk Railway had been confiscating carloads for its own use. The GTR's action of holding up inbound trains at border cities so it could carry out seizures had created such a backup of rail traffic in the United States that American railroad companies had declared an embargo against Canadian railroads. The embargo would remain in effect "until such times as the Canadian lines move freight more freely [permitting] the American lines to get some relief from the worst congestion they have ever experienced."

The problem with the GTR was resolved and the trains from the United States again began to arrive at Canadian terminals. Canadian railroads cut back on passenger service to make space for coal cars, to expedite distribution to shivering communities. In Guelph, coal dealers were granted an exemption from the Sabbath Observance bylaw so they could make deliveries on Sundays. However, for some the relief from the coal shortage was only temporary.

In the United States, factories and businesses were required to observe new "Heatless Days" regulations to conserve coal. That meant closing down on certain days of the week. Washington didn't demand that Ottawa follow suit, but there was an unspoken suggestion that out of "common decency" Canadian businesses should make the same sacrifice for the cause as their American friends. The Canadian government obligingly issued heatless days regulations.

In the first week of February, Guelph city hall acted on instructions from Ottawa. All factories and places of business were to be closed on Saturday, Sunday and Monday. Among the few exemptions were doctors' offices, drug stores and factories doing essential war work. The suddenness of the order caught the city by surprise, but few people opposed it. "There is a willing feeling to conform with the new regulations cheerfully," the newspaper said.

Problems that arose within hours were quickly solved by compromise. A grocer expressed his concern that farmers making their regular Saturday morning trip to town might not have heard of the new regulations. They would arrive after a long trip in their sleighs and wagons only to find shop doors locked, and would have to return home without goods their families needed. Grocery stores, bakeries and butcher shops were therefore allowed to be open Saturday until noon. Theatre managers were allowed to open on Saturday, their busiest day, but would have to close on Tuesday.

On the first Saturday that the new regulations were in effect, the newspaper noted that downtown Guelph had a "Sabbath-like appearance" because relatively few people were out and about. Restaurants, dry goods stores, florists, tobacconists and confectioners were shut up tight. The rotunda of the YMCA was open, but not the showers or the recreational facilities. Banks were "almost closed," admitting only clients who had due bills to pay. City Hall was closed on Monday, and all the heat shut off. The only exception was the office of Coal Controller Thomas Foster, who had to be available to receive government updates on the coal situation, and relay the news to the public.

In mid-February six railway cars full of coal arrived in Guelph; enough for about two weeks. Hundreds of people lined up at City Hall, waiting their turn to get a permit from the Coal Controller to buy half a ton. Many of the men had taken time off work, sacrificing a few hours' pay so their homes could be warm again. A police constable separated men and women into two lines. He was there to maintain order, but the people waiting in the cold were patient and cheerful. The paper reported, "Neither is the color line to be drawn in the coal line. All are treated alike, and the white citizen, be he a financier or a laborer, gets just the same privilege when he lines up as his yellow or dusky brother."

While the coal supply was a principal concern during the winter, supplemental food production was a major issue during the warmer months. Canadian wheat, corn, oats and other staples were feeding the Allied armies and millions of civilians, not to mention the innumerable horses and mules used by the military. The war's drain on food meant scantily stocked grocery store shelves.

In 1917 the Canadian Department of Agriculture launched the Vacant Lot Gardening campaign. To supplement farm production, city folk were encouraged to grow food not only for their own tables, but also to help feed the hungry population of Mother England. Guelphites who didn't have yards in which to plant gardens could apply to the city's Vacant Lot Committee for a piece of ground to cultivate. Members of the Guelph Horticultural Society volunteered their time to assist people with no gardening experience. Schoolchildren, housewives and the elderly did much of the work. Men who, for whatever reasons, had not "donned the khaki," put in time in the gardens after work hours and on weekends. Collectively, the gardens turned out a bountiful harvest of potatoes, carrots, onions, tomatoes and other vegetables. By the end of 1917, the Department of Agriculture had declared Guelph's "Vacant Lot Gardening Club" the "Best in the Dominion." Guelph had the greatest number of gardens of any city of comparable size in the country. But evidently not *everybody* in Guelph had been doing their bit.

On February 28, 1918, the local newspaper ran an article admonishing golfers and lawn bowlers for not giving up their fields for the cause. The paper had earlier reported that the golf links at Glace Bay in Cape Breton had produced six thousand bushels of potatoes. Why were the Guelph links not put to such practical use? Why indeed were some Guelph men dallying at games when they could be helping to grow the food that could well be the key to victory?

The paper said that men who weren't too old and feeble to bowl and play golf, weren't too old and feeble to cultivate a garden. The newspaper went so far as to charge that any physically fit man with leisure time who didn't help to cultivate the soil would be branded "a slacker, a traitor, and a betrayer of our soldiers and seamen."

The paper added, "If it be true that Drake was playing bowls when the Armada hove in sight, he dropped them till the Spaniards were defeated!"

It was finally determined that the grounds of Guelph's only golf course, the nine-hole Guelph Country Club; and those of the Guelph Lawn Bowling Club, were not particularly well-suited to the cultivation of vegetables, and so were not dug up. Some members of both clubs were serving overseas. Those who remained at home were active in raising funds for organizations like the Red Cross.

The war touched every family in Guelph, some more cruelly than others. Like the people of every other community, Guelphites tried to maintain a semblance of normalcy in the face of uncertainty and grief. But the war had pervaded every aspect of daily life, and was almost impossible to escape. Local sports leagues still provided the public with hockey, baseball, football and cricket games, as well as curling matches and track and field events. But dozens of familiar athletes were missing. Families could go for Sunday picnics in Riverside Park, but uniformed men could be seen everywhere. Some were returned men with missing limbs; others were new recruits spending what might well be a last weekend with loved ones.

Military parades helped keep public morale and the patriotic spirit high. Recruiting officers also hoped that the sight of proud young soldiers marching in step would encourage other youths to enlist. The soldiers would be accompanied by brass bands, Boy Scout troops, public school cadets, representatives of social clubs and local dignitaries. The parades would end in a park where the people enjoyed food and drinks while listening to patriotic speeches. A parade would be held to celebrate a visit from an important personage such as the Governor General of Canada, or to mark the anniversary of a battle. In April 1916, Guelphites crowded the downtown area to watch a parade in honour of the men who had fought at St. Julien a year earlier.

A month later, Guelphites were treated to a mock military exercise when the city became a training ground in what the newspaper called a "bloodless battle" with "imaginary shells bursting over Guelph."

The men of the 55th Overseas Battery advanced on Guelph from the north. Their objective was an imaginary artillery unit located near the Church of Our Lady on Catholic Hill, the highest point in the city. The 55th "dug in" near Eramosa Road, where trees shielded them from the view of enemy airplanes. Officers on horseback rode out to reconnoiter. On their instructions, made with flags because they didn't have telephones, the gunners determined the range of the target.

"At this juncture," said the report, "operations were suspended and the members of the battery had a first rate lunch of hot pork and beans, washed down with hot tea . . .

Horses were watered, fed and tethered to the gun carriages."

The exercise resumed after lunch. The 55th "fired" on the enemy position, but observing officers decided that the battery had taken a hit by the enemy's return fire. The artillery crews had to move their guns to a new location, from which they resumed their salvos, this time "destroying" their target. The men returned to their barracks where a hot dinner was waiting. The paper was pleased to report there had been no casualties; not even a horse losing a shoe.

Soldiers made up a large part of the downtown crowds on Friday and Saturday nights. Dances were popular, but officially "dry." The government had imposed prohibition as a temporary wartime measure, but beer and liquor could be had if you knew where to go.

Despite the presence of so many young soldiers on weekend leave looking for fun and excitement, rowdyism was relatively rare in Guelph. The soldiers were under strict orders to behave like gentlemen. On occasions when civilian youths engaged in street fights, constables quickly intervened and hauled them off to spend a night in a cell. In the morning they faced a magistrate who would give them the choice of a fine or a spell in the county jail. The war offered a third option: avoid fines and jail by volunteering for service overseas, where, as one judge put it, "You can get all the fighting you want." Those who chose enlistment were immediately escorted to the Armoury by a constable, before they had time to change their minds.

Among Guelph's most popular venues for public entertainment were the Apollo Theatre on Wyndham Street, Griffin's Opera House on Woolwich Street, and, as of October 1917, the new state-of-the-art Regent Theatre on Macdonell Street. The Regent boasted leather seats, marble floors and a "special" overhead fan imported from Chicago. Griffin's presented live plays staged by touring companies, but the principal attraction in all three theatres was the cinema. Soldiers and civilians crowded in to watch silent screen stars like comedian Charlie Chaplin, cowboy hero William S. Hart, Canadian-born Mary Pickford and even Guelph's own William Courtleigh.

Through the silver screen, audiences had the unprecedented opportunity to see actual images of the distant war in which their husbands, sons and brothers were fighting. They were awed by scenes of Allied soldiers in trenches going "over the top" in charges across no man's land amidst bursting shells and clouds of smoke. They weren't aware that many of these supposedly authentic battle scenes were in fact staged by British film production companies for propaganda purposes.

If Canadians had any doubts about the evil nature of the enemy, those were likely put to rest by *The Kaiser: The Beast of Berlin*, an American film whose cast included such rising stars as Elmo Lincoln and Lon Chaney. Advertisements for the movie labelled Kaiser Wilhelm as "The Murderer of Womanhood, Humanity, Youth, Civilization and Freedom."

The newspaper arranged showings at Griffin's of *The Battle of Courcelette* and *Advance of the Tanks*. The engagement at Courcelette was part of the Somme offensive of the summer of 1916, and up to that time the biggest battle the CEF had been in. The paper promised its readers that the film would show them "actual warfare at close range." They would experience "everything but the noise."

"History will set forth the facts," said the advance promotion. "Courcelette will rank higher than Queenston Heights in 1812, higher than Lundy's Lane, higher than Ridgeway in

'66, higher than Batoche in '85, or Paardeburg in 1900 . . . There were twice as many Canadians at Courcelette as there were British under Wellington at Waterloo. Next week at Griffin's Theatre in this city will be presented vivid official and authentic moving pictures of the Battle of Courcelette, the greatest film of the war for the eyes of the people of this country, for it shows the Canadians in action."

The companion film gave audiences a first look at the Allies' fearsome new weapon, "the wonderful tanks," in action. "They look like nothing one has ever seen before." A dramatic newspaper ad featured an illustration of a tank with its gun turrets blazing, rolling over the barbed wire in front of an enemy trench. Hapless German soldiers in the picture are cut down or throw up their hands in surrender.

War as it Really Is, a pioneering 1916 documentary, covered a wider scope of the war. Audiences were amazed by aerial views taken by pilots showing warships at Salonika, Greece. They saw brief but stunning footage of fighter plane combat. Astounding scenes of the Western Front showed artillery crews in action, and German prisoners being marched away under guard. A principal scene was the massive eruption of earth that came when the Allies detonated tons of dynamite their tunnellers had planted under German lines. The silent violence on the screen was spectacular, and for many in the audience brought home the reality of the hellish world in which their loved ones were fighting. It didn't look at all like the jolly time the men of the 55th Overseas Battery had that day when they fought the Battle of Guelph.

Voluntary enlistment dropped sharply after newspapers began publishing alarmingly long casualty lists. Recruiting posters like this one were part of a drive to shame reluctant young men into enlisting. (Library and Archives Canada C-147822)

CHAPTER 17

CONSCRIPTION: A ROUGH NIGHT FOR SOCIALISTS

"Brave Young Guelphites Do Not Want to Have Duty Presented," a Guelph headline sarcastically announced on November 28, 1916. In the article that followed, two army recruiters, Sergeants Laycock and Bryan, told a reporter of the difficulties they were having convincing young men to enlist. "One could hardly form a very high opinion of the quality of the young manhood from this city," the reporter lamented.

"We've only got one man yet," Laycock said, "and some of the excuses that we meet with are enough to make the heart of a man sick . . . One chap told me that he did not think it was up to him to go yet. Another fellow told me that he was certain that the shock would kill his mother. It does beat all, the love that some of these young men are developing nowadays for their parents, especially their mothers.

Another young fellow told me that his feet were bad. He didn't say they were cold, but that may have been the case."

Bryan picked up from his partner. "The greatest thing that we have to contend with is the absolute indifference of many of the men. Both Laycock and I are married men with families, and we know what we are talking about when we tell young men that it is their duty to enlist. Why, on Sunday night we stopped a group of eight or so in front of the opera house, and asked them if they did not think it was about time they were going to the front to help out the boys that had been there for many months now. Their reply was that if the fellows who wanted to go had gone and had been wounded or killed, that was their own look out and that it was nothing to them at all."

Recruiters like the two sergeants didn't just wait behind a desk for volunteers to come to them; they patrolled downtown Guelph, looking for potential soldiers. They found that the theatres were good places to catch young men not in uniform. At first the sergeants were permitted to stand in front of the audiences to appeal on behalf of king and country.

"But apparently the movie fans have no great liking for recruiting speeches," the paper said. "They like to see their heroes in films only."

The theatre managers complained that the recruiters were hurting business. Young men were staying away, and some patrons said they wouldn't come back as long as the recruiting speeches continued. Managers said they would show slides or do anything else to be of assistance, but they could no longer allow recruiters to speak to audiences. Bryan said they would never fill the battalions until the country had "some sort of compulsion."

Recruiters all over the country felt the same frustration. After the initial war fervour of 1914 and '15 had subsided, enlistment dropped off sharply. Guelph men like Harold J. Anderson, Alexander Carey, Ernest Colley, James Doughty and Charles H. Stewart signed up, but many others didn't agree that they had a "duty" to fight. Some believed family responsibilities came first. Others didn't think Germany posed any real threat to Canada, and even argued that Britain could have kept out of it. Most didn't see why they should give up their jobs or their studies to lay their lives on the line in a European war that, from their perspective, had nothing to do with them. They didn't consider themselves unpatriotic or cowardly.

But a government in desperate need to fill the depleted ranks on the Western Front thought differently. The "compulsion" Sergeant Bryan spoke of burst into newspaper columns and Canadian consciousness with the word *conscription*.

The Borden government's announcement that it intended to make military service compulsory for eligible male citizens was immediately divisive. Guelph families that already had husbands and sons serving with the CEF thought it was about time the young "slackers" in town were made to do their part. Others thought conscription a despotic measure worthy of the tyrannical regime in Germany. Guelph journalist Herb Philp, in one of his letters from the Western Front, expressed disgust for young men who had to be forced to fight for their country:

> I am glad to see them pressing the gallant
> procrastinators into service. Personally, I
> shall take just as much delight in giving
> them quite as lusty a hurrah at their arrival

as they gave us at our departure. They may
not be of much use in the front line, but
at least there is ample work to do mending
roads at the back of the front, so that the
fighting lads can have a decent rest when
they come out. God forgive me if I am trying
to pass judgement upon others, but when I
see the grey-haired, aye, and white-haired
old lads who have come out here in the navy
battalions, I sometimes cannot help thinking
that these sleek shirkers at home are failing
us beyond endurance; and that they have
forfeited their right to the name British.

Months before Parliament could pass legislation on
conscription, the order went out for bachelors and child-
less widowers between the ages of twenty and thirty-four
to register for the draft or apply for legal exemption by
November 10, 1917. The newspaper reported a sudden
increase in the number of young Canadian men crossing
into the United States at Niagara Falls, Windsor and Sarnia.
A Windsor correspondent wrote, "Attracted by high wages,
especially in the Detroit automobile factories, and actuated
in part by desire for relief from persistent recruiting appeals,
great numbers of Canadians have crossed here to take up
residence on the other side of the boundary."

At Sarnia alone, fifteen hundred Canadian men crossed the
border in the period of one fortnight. While Canadian border
authorities looked at them with contempt, their American counterparts found the situation amusing. "What are you coming
over here for? Are you afraid of conscription in Canada?"
became standard questions. Answers were usually evasive.

Recruiting officers like Guelph's Captain Reverend William Hindson, who had been denied the opportunity to serve overseas, tried their utmost to convince reluctant youths that it would be far better for them to volunteer than wait to be conscripted. Volunteers were heroes, admired by all. But there was a negative stigma to being a conscript.

Hindson was one of the organizers of a recruiting rally held in Griffin's Opera House on the evening of April 14, 1917. The principal speaker was Captain Reverend Alexander MacGillivray. He said it was a shame and a humiliation for Guelph to have to hold a recruiting meeting at that stage of the war. He received loud applause when he expressed scorn for men who "had little manhood in them. Their hearts must be impregnable to the call for justice . . . We are not fighting for anything except the freedom of the whole world, and the existence of our Empire."

MacGillivray asked how any eligible young man could look a returned soldier in the face without dropping his head in shame. "Have you no pride, no patriotism, no gratitude . . . They did your dirty work, and now it is up to you to go and do your own."

Some of the returned soldiers, MacGillivray said, had lain wounded on the battlefield for hours and hours before being found. "Today, owing to the splendid organization of the Medical Corps, a man is no sooner wounded, than he is cared for, and it has been known where a wounded man was on his way back to a comfortable hospital in England 18 hours after being wounded."

After that reassuring statement, Hindson stepped up to the podium. He told the audience that they were living in the greatest days in the history of the world. "The old order of things is passing away, never to return . . . The call of duty, honor and chivalry, and of God has come. If there is a young man who is not ready to respond to that call now, I can only say that he will forever be ashamed."

The stirring speeches were published in the newspaper. In the days and weeks that followed, Sergeants Bryan and Laycock were no doubt pleased to see more young Guelphites report for duty. But it was still just a trickle. Moreover, many eligible men not only rejected the call to volunteer, but also ignored the order to register.

Early in November, with the deadline looming, the paper reported that sixty per cent of Guelph's eligible men had failed to register. Magistrate Lewis M. Hayes received a letter from the military registrar in London that would have gone out to judges all over Canada. It stated that civilian police departments would be given instructions concerning evaders of the *Military Service Act*. The paper said the slackers were in for a rude awakening. Eligible men who failed to register would be treated as deserters. Chief Randall was given a list of between 350 and 400 names of men who would be subject to arrest if they did not register immediately. This threat evidently had the desired effect.

It became mandatory for men to carry their registration certificates, their certificates of exemption or their marriage certificates with them at all times, and to present them to a constable on demand. Police would periodically raid places like movie theatres. In one such instance, patrons of Griffin's were told that city and Dominion police were waiting at the front door to check men's papers. All other exits were guarded. Only one man did not have the necessary paper. He was marched straight to the police station and spent the night in jail. The following morning he explained to a magistrate that he had registered, but had gone out without the certificate in his pocket. He was released with a warning not to repeat the offence.

Citizens who supported the war were exasperated by those who did not. Most bewildering of all were the socialists, whose philosophy seemed to be contrary to all that was held dear to those who believed in a capitalist economy, Protestant morality and British Imperialism. Leaders of the socialist movement in Canada had been outspoken in their opposition to the war, and now they took up the anti-conscription cause.

On the evening of May 31, 1917, Guelph's Trades and Labour Hall on Macdonell Street was jam-packed for a meeting that had been called by the local branch of the Social Democratic Party. Waiting to step up to the platform to give voice to their views on conscription were Albert Farley and Lorne Cunningham of Guelph, and Mervin Smith of Kitchener. In its report, the paper would precede these men's names with "Comrade." A hostile atmosphere pervaded the room, because few of those present were socialist sympathizers. According to the paper, "Active soldiers, returned soldiers, Liberals, Conservatives, Independents, Socialists, Protestants, Catholics, Home Rulers, anti-Home Rulers, lawyers, laborers, Jews and Gentiles were all represented." Guelph had been rife with rumours that if the socialists persisted in holding the meeting, there would be trouble. Undoubtedly, some men were there in anticipation of a brawl. Several police constables were in attendance, likely because the previous Saturday a socialist anti-conscription meeting in Kitchener at which Smith had spoken had ended in a riot.

Farley, the chairman of the meeting, was the first to speak:

> I am glad to see so many here to discuss the question of conscription. I believe it is the most serious question that has ever come before the people of Canada in its history. There has been talk around town today of there being trouble here tonight. We are not children any longer. We want to discuss this thing from the stand point of men. If you do not consider what we have to say is right, you have a perfect right to consider it as you see it. I ask you to respect our beliefs and the way we view the subject.

A few boos and hisses came from the crowd, but Farley continued:

> You take the way this thing has shaped up, when it is a question among the officials as to whether we have a right to hold this meeting . . . It puts me in mind [of a story] of the dog crossing the river with a bone in its mouth, and it saw its shadow and let go of the bone to grasp the one it saw in the shadow . . . we should be very careful that we don't make the mistake that the dog did. It may be possible we might be losing a real liberty in place of a shadow . . . I ask you men to discuss this thing and listen in a reasonable way.

The crowd remained restrained as Cunningham took his turn to speak. He said that if he believed in war, militarism, the capitalist system; and if he believed "that the present war was brought about for the sole avowed purpose for which the leaders in the various countries that has [*sic*] brought about this war say it is against human liberty, I would not at the present time be here . . . I would have been recruited in the first batch that left Guelph."

A heckler shouted, "Seeing is believing. Why don't you go and see?"

Cunningham responded with a lengthy discourse on the history of socialism, capitalism, the British Empire and the class struggle between the haves and the have-nots. "I think it can be safely claimed that every war in the history of mankind within the last five or six centuries at least, has been a war for economic supremacy."

Backing his arguments with quoted figures, Cunningham explained that capitalists kept the lion's share of the wealth produced by the working class and manipulated supply and demand in such a way that it was to their advantage to periodically slow down production and lay workers off. "It means you must sit idly by until they can find an investment . . . and then you begin to work again."

Cunningham used American tycoon John D. Rockefeller as an example of the unfairness of the system. He said he had nothing against Rockefeller personally. "He is a very good Baptist gentleman as far as I know. [But] Some years ago his income was reckoned at $68,000,000 . . . It could feed the working class of the entire world."

And yet, Cunningham said, even without war there were hard times in which working men couldn't feed their children. When a war like the present one broke out, he continued, capitalists profited from it, placing patriotism second to the accumulation of more wealth, while working men were forced to don the uniforms of their countries and fight for the capitalist "masters."

The crowd listened patiently until Cunningham said, "Consequently we are opposed to the war and for that reason we are opposed to being forced to defend the country. This doesn't apply to the men in khaki. They already know where they are at . . . Personally, conscription may come. I might be physically unfit. It doesn't make any difference."

Someone shouted, "Hope you can't."

"Whether I am or not," Cunningham said, "I'd refuse on that basis to don the khaki and fight."

Another voice cried, "Shut up!"

Sensing the growing animosity, Cunningham defended his right to speak. "I am sure it is not necessary for us to have a hub-bub . . . that the hall would be smashed up and everything else. I don't look as if I would harm anybody."

"No chance!" a man shouted. Another said, "What are we in khaki for? We are fighting for you."

Cunningham tried to continue with his condemnation of the "enemy of the working class." But there were catcalls, and the crowd's restlessness took hold. Chairman Farley called for order. A soldier responded with, "Free speech for everybody," and told Farley to sit down and mind his own business. Then Cunningham and Farley faced what the paper called a "Shrapnel of Questions."

"What are our boys fighting for?" one man asked. "The capitalist class, or for the freedom of our wives and children?"

The paper reported only that Cunningham's answer was unsatisfactory. A soldier fired off angrily, "You ain't got spunk enough in you to fight for them. Look at the honour roll of your own union organization. Why aren't you up there, and the chairman also?"

"Give us a chance," Farley pleaded. "You are a man, so am I."

A voice cut him short. "And some of us have a lot to say.

We are after conscription, for the simple reason that we have sympathy for the thousands who have lost their lives . . . You wouldn't fight for liberty. You would crawl into a hole . . . the war wasn't started until Germany went through Belgium and we saw that women were raped and children's hands cut off. Is that a commercial war?"

The atmosphere in the room grew ever more heated as volleys of words were exchanged. Then, tiring of listening to Farley and Cunningham, the crowd began to cry, "Give us Smith!" According to the newspaper report, the soldiers said they would chase him out of Guelph just as he had been chased out of Kitchener.

Smith was visibly nervous as he took the platform to a mingling of cheers and jeers. A hush came over the audience when he began to speak. Smith said that capitalism was to blame for the war. "I joined the socialist party for the purpose of throwing all my energies against such conditions that make wars unavoidable. And because the war has come, I do not think I should change my opinion and position . . . War is here and the horrors of war as some of you men know, but that was the opinion I came to and because of these opinions I am still against war."

Voices shouted, "Conscientious objector! Shame on you!"

Smith argued that he didn't see why he should offer himself in the interests of capitalism. He said he believed in the cause of the working class. "If I can give up my life in the interests of socialism, alright [sic]. I decided that years ago, and it doesn't move me in the slightest."

"You're a hero," someone called out derisively.

Smith responded that a man could be a hero in more ways than one. He said that they (socialists) were not like the Nationalists in Quebec (who were strongly opposed to conscription), or the people who opposed conscription on religious grounds. Their fight was with the capitalist system that made the working people of different countries fight each other for the financial interests of the wealthy.

Again, the words flew hot and heavy. When Farley attempted to intercede, he was shouted down. One man accused Smith of feeling sorry for Germany. He replied that he felt sorry for German working people, but not German capitalists. Someone else asked if Smith would protect his own wife and family.

"I certainly would," he replied, "and there would be a reason. I can't understand why, in order to protect my wife and family, I have to go out and shoot the husband of some other family . . . the destruction of homes and the killing of women and children have nothing to do with war or why I am opposed to them."

A soldier asked Smith why he wouldn't take up arms against a country that was going to invade Canada. Smith said no country was going to invade Canada. At that, a returned soldier hotly responded that a German prisoner had told him Germany was going to run the world; that she would win the war by foul means; that after defeating France and England, she would invade Canada. "Do you mean to say you wouldn't take up arms and fight for your country, the country you get your liberty from?"

Another soldier shouted for Smith to "Get in the defence force." As he continued to state his case, there were cries of "Liar!" and angry remarks that he didn't know what it was like at the front and probably didn't have any friends there. "Why don't you slide down into the trenches . . . We are at war with Germany." Some soldiers started singing "It's a Long Way to Tipperary."

The confrontation came to a head after Smith was asked what he would do if a German came along and cut his daughter's hands off, and he replied that he would not want to make it possible for wars to create such conditions. He was then asked if he was in favour of conscripting the country's wealth. Smith said he would be, if it was in the interest of the working classes.

A soldier asked, "Are we not in the working classes?"

"Yes," Smith replied.

Then a soldier demanded to know why the socialists didn't help them with conscription.

Smith shot back, "Why didn't you help us stop the war before the war ever came? That is all I have to say."

Someone shouted, "We are going to have conscription." There were cries of "Hurrah! Hurrah!" from the audience. Smith said, "When the war is over, you will be on the socialists' side." The crowd burst into laughter.

Someone in the audience started singing the national anthem, and the soldiers boisterously joined in. The socialist speakers didn't participate. Smith had stepped down from the platform, but a soldier told him to get back up and sing "God Save the King." He refused.

A man identified in the report only as "Comrade Hill of Guelph" attempted to speak up for Smith. The soldiers decided to make him join Smith in a duet. They hauled the two men onto the platform and called for anyone who could play to accompany them on the hall's piano.

The first volunteer pianist banged away with one finger so badly that another shoved him aside, saying, "How do you expect a man to sing to such playing as that?" But the second would-be musician's hammering on the keys was no better. A third was found who could produce a recognizable tune. Meanwhile, Hill and Smith looked, in the words of the reporter, "as though they were halting between opinions. Whether to go over the parapet or surrender."

A hundred soldiers surrounded the platform, blocking any chance of escape. The constables in the hall didn't rush to the rescue. They stood on their chairs so they could see over the soldiers' heads. Newspaper reporters took notes from a safe place behind the piano. Trapped and scared, Smith and Hill sang "God Save the King," and the soldiers sang with them. Then, the paper reported, "The hall was cleared and the stage set outdoors for the after meeting."

Out on the street, the soldiers hastily organized a procession, with Farley, Cunningham, Smith, Hill and a few other known local socialists at the head. They were forced to lead a parade along Wyndham Street, followed by rowdy soldiers and a large number of civilians. A crowd of onlookers watched them pass through St. George's Square. The procession stopped in front of Griffin's Opera House. The soldiers tried to gain entry to the theatre so they could put their hapless captives on stage for all to see. The manager would have none of it, and this time the constables moved in to protect private property. But they left the socialists in the hands of the mob.

While the soldiers were wondering what to do next, a light rain began to fall. No one in the "parade" had a raincoat except Smith, who had managed to put it on before he was hustled out of the Trades and Labour Hall. The soldiers ordered him to take it off and carry it, saying that if they could stand the rain, so could he.

The socialists were marched downtown again, this time to the front of the King Edward Hotel. There, Cunningham, Smith and Farley, in turn, suffered the indignity of being tossed in the air with a blanket while the crowd cheered. When the soldiers tired of that game, they again forced the three to sing "God Save the King," and then to shout "Three cheers for conscription."

The soldiers wanted to give the blanket treatment to another man, James Smith (no relation to Mervin), who had allegedly been one of the organizers of the anti-conscription meeting. They were disappointed to learn that he had given them the slip back at the hall, and had then disappeared. Smith was a barber whose shop was on the King Edward Hotel premises. When hotel manager James Johnson heard that the crowd intended to smash up the shop, he went out and prevailed upon them to refrain from damaging hotel property. There were murmurs about paying a visit to Smith's home, but as the hour was now late, the crowd dispersed, leaving the socialists rattled, wet and supposedly chastised.

The newspaper reported that James Smith had sought sanctuary at a friend's house. He didn't open his barber shop the next morning after being advised by friends that it wouldn't be wise. He received a notice from Johnson to vacate the premises. The paper said that after the reception Mervin Smith had received in Guelph, it would probably be a long time before he visited the city again.

The paper admitted that the soldiers had been unruly, but couldn't blame men who had "smelt the powder" for having little patience with "theorists" who established their views from the safety of home. The socialist meeting and what followed, said the report, was "real, red-hot, yard-wide drama and tragedy" that was better entertainment than any movie, and didn't cost spectators a cent to watch. The newspaper said it was "one of the most exciting nights in the history of the city."

A wagon representing Guelph Carpet Mills about to join the armistice parade in 1918. Guelph's first street celebration of the war's end turned out to be premature. (Courtesy of Guelph Museums 1990.2.5)

CHAPTER 18
WAR NEWS 1918

In the early days of July 1918, nothing indicated that the war would end anytime soon. The United States had entered the conflict, bringing fresh troops and its economic and industrial might to the Allied cause. But an earth-shaking revolution had taken Russia out of the war, freeing many German soldiers that had been tied up on the Eastern Front to reinforce the army locked in the stalemate on the Western Front. The great Allied offensives of previous summers, that had held great promise of final victory, had bogged down in the mud and carnage of the Somme and Passchendaele. New promises that 1918 would be different were met with skepticism. Newspaper editorials speculated that the fighting would carry on into 1919 and even 1920.

Support for the war remained strong, largely because a weary public wanted to get it over with. Conscription, undreamed of in the early months, was dividing Canadians at every level, from Parliament Hill in Ottawa to homes in communities like Guelph. War profiteering had blighted the national pride Canadians took from the accomplishments of the heroes at the front. Most distressing of all, in the four years since the flag-waving and drum-beating of 1914, had been the long and ongoing list of obituaries for fallen soldiers. If you hadn't lost a loved one, chances were good that you knew a family that had. And you couldn't help but notice returned soldiers like Guelph's Arthur McQuillan, who came home without his left arm.

Stories about deteriorating conditions in Germany and the chaotic situation in Russia took up almost as much front page space as reports on the Western Front. Guelphites read that the starving German population had grown disenchanted with the Kaiser and were being stirred up by socialists. But the politicians and generals had been predicting Germany's imminent collapse since 1914. Now they were also saying that the Bolsheviks who had overthrown the Russian czar couldn't last very long.

Letters written by soldiers serving overseas and published in the local paper were fewer and farther between. Formerly they had been a major feature, published regularly under "From the Firing Line." They had included vivid eyewitness accounts of trench warfare from correspondents like Herb Philp.

Now they appeared only occasionally, placed, it would seem, where column space was available. The heading simply said: "Soldiers' Letters." Some still carried revealing anecdotes about war action, such as Captain James D. Doughty's description of the first aerial dogfight he had ever witnessed:

Just above me I saw a German and an English airplane chasing one another. Our plane seemed to be on top, when all of a sudden it took a nose dive. I thought it was hit and was falling, but it came down below the German plane and was firing at it with the machine gun, and by good luck the German plane was hit. Down it fell in a circular movement. We all ran over to it, but it was burning before we got there, and we could not save the German pilot and had to let him burn. No doubt he was killed before he hit the ground.

Doughty said he was looking forward to the day he would get home to "good old Canadian weather and food."

Other letter writers spoke of more mundane matters, such as the soldier who wanted his mother to let people know about the good work the YMCA was doing in France, keeping the men's morale up by providing chocolate, biscuits, cigarettes and tins of milk. "We are all getting fat," he wrote. War fatigue might have contributed to the decline in the number of soldiers' letters the paper published. Perhaps, after four years, they had little to say that hadn't already been said. Perhaps fewer families were willing to pass their correspondence on to the newspaper. Many local men whose letters had been shared with the whole town through the newspaper were now dead. A letter might well be the final words to a family, and therefore better kept private.

That July of 1918, while Guelphites went about their daily affairs under the unmoving cloud of war, momentous events were shaking the Western Front. Since March, the Germans had been on the offensive, trying to break the stalemate and win the war before the Americans could arrive in force. The Allies had retreated before the horrific onslaught, giving up more ground than either side had lost or gained in the entire war. To the German high command, victory seemed within their grasp.

But the German army became over-extended. It was unable to sustain the attack and consolidate its gains. It faltered. In mid-July the Allies struck back with a series of counterattacks that sent the exhausted Germans reeling back across the recently captured ground. The Allies now had the momentum and determined to keep the pressure on. On August 8, the Canadians and Australians, who had been held in reserve, took their place at the front of the Allied thrust. It was a position to which they had become accustomed after many months of hard experience.

By 1918, the "colonials" had earned a reputation as fearsome "shock troops" that were devastatingly effective at spearheading attacks. While the Australians were notorious for a swaggering cockiness, the Canadians had been characterized by raw self-confidence and a grim, bone-deep desire to get the rotten job of war done with so they could go home.

Back in Guelph and other hometowns, newspapers had proudly reported that German prisoners told interrogators that their generals would reinforce any sector at which it appeared the Canadians were about to attack. They said German troops in their trenches feared the Canadians and their bayonets more than any other Allied soldiers.

The Canadian attack that started near Amiens on August 8 drove the Germans back more than twelve kilometres.

The date would go down in German military annals as "The Black Day." It was the beginning of what would come to be known as "The Hundred Days"; the spectacular final phase of the war. The Canadians would win one victory after another: at Arras, Canal du Nord, Cambrai, Denain, Valenciennes and Mons. But stiff German resistance resulted in the CEF's worst casualty rate of the war. In August alone, 4,563 Canadians died. Another 4,548 were killed in September. Thousands more men were wounded or reported missing in action.

Guelphites might have taken initial reports of the stunning German reversals with a degree of skepticism. They'd read similar accounts before, only to have high hopes dashed by disappointment. But this time, as the weeks crept by, there were no accounts of "setbacks," or stories about German claims to phantom victories. Anyone who read the paper and looked at a map of the Western Front could see that the German lines were indeed collapsing.

"Go Anywhere with Canadians," boasted a headline on August 17. "Imperialists Eager to Work with Canucks In Tank Brigades — 'Put On Greatest Show Ever Seen In the War' Say British."

Finally, as the Canadians "covered themselves in glory," there was reason to hope that the end of the war was in sight. But any excitement Guelphites might have felt over the prospect was subdued. The good news of victory was always followed by the tally of the cost in blood. Hardly a day passed without casualty reports in the local paper.

On August 21, it reported the deaths of Phillip Peer, Jack Samuels, Melville Bonus and John Mitchell. On September 4 the city learned that Patrick Keleher and Victor Henderson were dead. James Doughty, whose letter had so recently been published in the paper, was among the numerous Guelph soldiers reported wounded.

In that same September 4 edition, the paper quoted an unnamed Allied general (referring to him only as "one of our great chiefs") who'd said, "The hour seems close at hand when superb efforts of the Allies will begin to bear fruit. We are on the last lap and close to the winning post." The paper also brought attention to the vital work done by the merchant marine, noting that fifteen thousand civilian sailors had been "murdered" by German U-boats and floating mines. "No life was ever more nobly given than by those unsung heroes who go down to the sea in ships."

The war at sea, which had to a degree been overshadowed in the press by the clash of armies on land, was brought back to the public's attention with the news that British and Canadian soldiers had stormed into battle with the cry of "Remember the *Llandovery Castle*" That was the vengeful response to the sinking on June 27, 1918, of a Canadian hospital ship and the machine-gunning of survivors. In the hearts and minds of Canadians, the attack on the *Llandovery Castle* ranked with the sinking of the *Lusitania* as a barbaric atrocity. In what once might have been considered a breach of censorship regulations, the Guelph paper told readers that secret plans for Canadian operations had been characterized as "the L.C. scheme."

The casualties among Guelph's soldiers mounted through September: Percy Smith, Edward Lobsinger, Percy Quartermain, Fred Kirvan, William Flemming. All of them dead. "This is the hardest blow that Guelph has sustained in a long time," said the paper, "and is ample evidence that the recent successful drive of the Allies was not won without many of our bravest falling."

The bittersweet news reports of victories and casualties continued without interruption into October. "Germans in Disorder" was the banner headline October 10. "Over a Million in Retreat Past Cambrai — Kaiser Reported to Have Abdicated." A front-page battlefield map illustrated the Allies' advance. But that month Guelph residents learned of the losses of Elvin Carter, Henry Aubrey Thompson, Walter Hayward, Roger Trendell and Chaplain Charles Ashbury Sparling.

November's news was at once exhilarating and confusing. From all accounts, the Germans were beaten. On November 7, a huge, bold-lettered headline announced, "WAR IS ENDED." The subtext, *Special to the Mercury*" said the Allies and Germany had signed an armistice that called for an end to the fighting at 2 p.m. that day. Other front page articles had conflicting information. One said that New York City was wild with joy over news of the war's end. Another said the news was unconfirmed, "But Feeling Is General that United Press Dispatches Are True."

Ecstatic Guelphites couldn't wait for confirmation. Church bells rang and factory whistles blew in celebration. People poured out of their homes and workplaces to swell the downtown crowds and give vent to four years of pent-up anxieties. Impromptu parades went up and down Wyndham Street, with joyful people waving Union Jacks and the Stars and Stripes. "It seemed that every motor car and truck in the city was out and decorated," said the newspaper. Students from the OAC joined the throng. Salvation Army musicians turned out with their instruments and were accompanied by people banging on tin pans and anything else that would make a noise.

The following day the paper remarked that Guelph was "a Great Little Celebrator." The newspaper reported that the crowd on Wyndham Street was so big it was impossible to walk through, and "Girls lost their hats in the melee."

But the good news was premature. Guelphites soon learned that even though the enemy's position was hopeless, German soldiers were still fighting, even using poison gas in a last-ditch defence of their homeland. The letdown was maddening. No one doubted that, any day now, there would be a genuine report of Germany's surrender. The great fear in Guelph households was that a son, husband or brother who by good luck or the grace of God had survived the war for months or even years, would be snatched away in its last days.

The news that Guelph and the rest of the world had been awaiting for so long finally came, and this time it was official. Germany and the Allies had agreed to an armistice. At eleven o'clock on the morning of November 11, four years of savage warfare came to an abrupt stop. An almost unnatural silence fell across the Western Front. Men had died up until the last minute. Private George Lawrence Price of Saskatchewan, picked off by a sniper at 10:58, was the last Canadian on record to be killed in action. The last Guelph man killed by enemy fire appears to have been Frank Henry, who was mortally wounded on October 31 when an artillery shell exploded near him while he was off-duty and walking down the street of a French village. Another Guelph soldier, John McTague, who had been taken prisoner, was released to the British, only to die of apparent heart failure on November 14. However, McTague's would not be the local paper's final war-related obituary.

A workshop in the Speedwell Convalescent Military Hospital, formerly a prison. Patients and nurses complained that it was understaffed, underfunded, and unsuited to its purpose. (Courtesy of Guelph Museums 1978.6.8)

CHAPTER 19
HOMECOMING

On the night of February 13, 1919, a returned soldier who was being held in the Guelph jail tried to commit suicide by slashing his wrist with a jackknife. He was found in time to be rushed to hospital. As a doctor stitched up his arm, the man sobbed, "Please don't send me to jail." He had lost a leg in France, and said he'd also suffered shell-shock. He'd been arrested for stealing a military medal from a fellow soldier, and had even had his own name engraved on it. The soldier couldn't explain why he had stolen the medal. A magistrate had initially sentenced him to sixty days in the county jail, but after the suicide attempt he reduced the sentence to one week. For many soldiers, the return to their old lives wasn't easy.

On November 12, 1918, the Guelph paper announced that some thirty-five thousand men of the CEF who were still in Canada would be disbanded almost immediately. "The maintenance of such a large number of men necessarily involves a huge expense, which will not be borne by the Government if the men are not required for service in France." Nonetheless, a few weeks later Acting Minister of Justice Arthur Meighen stated the government's intention to rigorously prosecute *Military Service Act* defaulters. The Dominion Police were instructed to apprehend all known offenders. The newspaper advised employers and others to "bear in mind that the regulations prohibiting the employment, harboring or assisting of defaulters, deserters and absences without leave, remains in full effect, and will be enforced."

The armistice of November 11 ended the fighting on the Western Front, but the war would not officially end until Germany and the Allies signed a peace treaty. (That did not come about until June 28, 1919, with the signing of the Treaty of Versailles.) There was still sporadic fighting on the Eastern Front because of the chaos brought about by the Russian Revolution. Newspaper editorials speculated that Germany might resist the harsh terms dictated by the victorious Allies. The families of men serving overseas wondered how much longer it would be before they could come home. The surviving volunteers of 1914 had been away from home for the full four years of the war.

In fact, returned soldiers had been arriving in Guelph since 1915. Although an officer might be granted a period of leave to visit his home, most of the returned men had been sent back because of wounds or illness. One of the earliest was Lance corporal Clifford Nourse. Born in South Africa, Nourse had been a student at the OAC when the war began. He enlisted immediately. By the spring of 1915 he was fighting in the deadly Ypres Salient. On a hazardous nighttime reconnaissance mission in which he had to crawl across no man's land to spy on German positions, Nourse was shot in the neck. He lay at the bottom of a trench for hours before stretcher-bearers found him.

Nourse was sent to a hospital in England, and was awarded the Distinguished Service Medal. Nerve damage had left one of his arms paralyzed, so he was put aboard the passenger steamer *Hesperian*, bound from Liverpool to Montreal. On September 4, 1915, the *Hesperian* was torpedoed by a German U-boat off the coast of Ireland. Thirty-two lives were lost, but Nourse was among the survivors. He eventually made it back to Canada, where his extraordinary adventures had already been described in the newspapers.

In early October, the paper learned that Nourse was in Guelph, visiting friends at the OAC. A reporter was dispatched to the college to track him down and get an exclusive interview. War hero tales made great copy.

The reporter found Nourse, but the hero was reluctant to talk about his experiences. His story "had to be fairly dragged out of him," as the reporter put it.

"Yes, I was wounded all right," Nourse said, "but it didn't amount to much, and I will be all right and back on the job again before long."

Nourse preferred to talk about the courage and sacrifices of other Canadian soldiers he had known, several of whom were former OAC students. Of the soldiers he'd shipped out with, Nourse said, "There are just a few left . . . they showed the stuff they were made of."

When asked to describe life in the trenches, Nourse shook his head. "I don't want to say anything about that."

It wasn't quite what the reporter wanted to hear, and returned soldiers would repeat words like it many times in the years to come.

Most returned soldiers made the Atlantic crossing without experiencing adventures like those of Clifford Nourse. But even though communities held joyous victory celebrations, many arrived in hometowns like Guelph with harrowing tales about conditions aboard some of the ships. Vessels were so crowded, that seriously wounded men who had been given special red tickets that entitled them to beds in cabins were instead sent to quarters deep in the hold where they lay on wet deck floors. Men complained that their quarters were foul-smelling and hot, the lavatories were disgustingly filthy, the food bad and the ships overrun with vermin. Some men said they went for days without the dressings on their wounds being changed. There were reports of officers making patients get off their cots and stand for daily drill, when they could barely stand at all. The complaints resulted in a closed-door Court of Inquiry held in Ottawa.

The Ontario Reformatory in Guelph was transformed into the Speedwell Convalescent Military Hospital, one of several institutions established by the federal and provincial governments to care for and rehabilitate sick and wounded soldiers so they could once again be useful, productive members of society. But for returned soldiers there were no grand homecoming welcomes to match the parades and celebrations that had seen them march off to war. Organizations like the Guelph Veterans' Association tried to help them re-adjust to "normal" life. But the government that had relentlessly called men to duty now became miserly in the treatment of veterans.

Speedwell's wards were full of men who had come home with crippling injuries. Some were psychologically shattered, often plagued with guilt because they had survived while others perished. The prison-turned-hospital was underfunded and understaffed. Nurses complained that they had to reuse hypodermic needles sterilized with water boiled in tin cans. The walls were poorly insulated, and ran with condensation in the fall and spring. Members of the administration were found to be incompetent. Convalescent soldiers resented the fact that Speedwell employed civilians who hadn't fought in the war, instead of unemployed returned soldiers; comrades-in-arms whom they believed better suited to working with veterans.

In March 1918, the newspaper informed the city that twenty-one "Guelph Originals" — men who had been among the first to volunteer in 1914 — would be returning home on a train from London. Eleven had been wounded, and the others were on temporary leave. The paper published the news of the arrival, and on the evening of March 20, hundreds of people waited at the station to welcome the heroes home. The crowd was so dense, "that several people were crushed, and one lady relative of one of the returning men fainted, and had to be carried into the station."

Mayor John Newstead and several of the city's aldermen were there to make the welcome official. But the paper had received inaccurate information. When the train rolled into the station, only one soldier stepped off. The other men were on a different train that arrived later that night, after everybody had gone home.

In downtown Guelph, in the parks, and at church, Guelphites came face to face with men with crutches and empty sleeves. It was distressing, but they were told that such was the sacrifice of war. They were told that these heroes had, at least, come home alive. A Guelph editorial even made a case for silver linings.

Under the heading "Victory Over Wounds: The Disabled Soldiers' Resurrection," an unnamed clergyman told of several men he knew who, before the war, had been employed at menial, low-paying jobs. They had come home from France with various disabilities: two with missing arms, one totally blind in one eye and partially blind in the other, and several described only as being "severely injured." Through occupational training at the convalescent hospitals, he said, these men had been able to secure better paying and more promising employment than they had ever thought possible before the war. "I am, technically, a better man all around," one of them said.

The newspaper advised Guelphites, "Have Patience with Soldiers." The accompanying article told of a conference the Methodist Church held in Hamilton at which the principal speaker was Major H.B. Clark, a returned army chaplain. Major Clark said returned soldiers would require patience and sympathy because they "had gone from a land where everything was prohibited to a land where everything is permitted." After living "the continental life," said the Major, it would be impossible for the men to immediately "settle into the niches of Canada, with its great Puritan ideals, of which we are all so proud."

But while clerics might have been concerned about the state of a man's moral fibre after exposure to the permissiveness of France, returned soldiers faced more worrisome problems. They had enlisted with the expectation that their old jobs would be waiting for them when they came home.

For some men, that was true. However, many factories had suspended domestic manufacturing in order to do war work. With the armistice, war production came to an almost immediate halt. There was no further need for the uniforms, munitions and military hardware that had kept the engines of industry running. It would take time to readjust to a peacetime economy.

Soldiers had been promised government pensions if they suffered debilitating injuries in their war service. By February 1918, veterans were already complaining that the Pensions Board wasn't dealing fairly with returned men. At a meeting held that month by the Guelph Branch of the Great War Veterans' Association, attendees heard that some men were receiving pensions as small as two dollars a month. It was just one of a steadily growing list of grievances.

Veterans were angry that the families of numerous deceased and invalidated soldiers had been reduced to depending on charity. The situation had been highlighted in the press by the case of a Toronto woman whose husband had come home from the war a total invalid. She couldn't care for him and their children on his tiny pension, and so went to work in a munitions factory. She was killed in a streetcar accident, leaving the children and their crippled father destitute.

Then there was the much-resented order from Ottawa that patients in Speedwell and the other convalescent military hospitals were to wear blue bands on their left arms whenever they left the premises. The bands were to be sewn onto their sleeves so they couldn't be removed. The order was a Canadian copy of a regulation in England that was imposed to prevent ambulatory patients of military convalescent hospitals from buying alcohol or drinking in pubs. A newspaper article provided a scenario of the reactions in hospitals like Speedwell when sergeants strode into the wards with the armbands and told the men to sew them onto their left sleeves.

"Immediately there arose a howl to the high heavens and protestations were hurled at the sergeant . . . I can't sew, sarge . . . I left that arm at Vimy, sarge . . . I have no needle and thread, sarge . . . How can a fellow with no right hand sew a band around his left arm, sarge?"

The men were told there would be consequences if they didn't obey the order. "That settled the matter, and there followed the greatest sewing-bee ever seen in Canada. At Whitby, Guelph, London, all over Canada from East to West, needles and thread were in demand. Regimental tailors were swamped in a minute, and men who could not sew were offering money, cigarettes and tobacco to skilled needle workers."

One disgruntled soldier gave his explanation for an order he and his comrades considered absurd. "Some wholesale cloth merchant had a lot of this blue stuff left on his hands, so he took a run up to Ottawa and worked his pull. Now he has sold his stock out, at a good price."

On April 19, 1918, a burly soldier dressed in the uniform of the Highlanders walked into the Guelph newspaper office. He startled everyone when he bellowed in a voice with a thick Scottish accent, "Do I look like a dead man?"

The soldier was Private George Leacock. He presented a copy of the paper from April 1915 that said he'd been killed in the Battle of Langemarck and was buried under a cross in Flanders. Leacock had been well known in Guelph, because he had a powerful bass voice and often sang at Griffin's Opera House.

Leacock explained to the newspaper staff that he'd been gassed at Langemarck, and lay in a shell hole for hours before British soldiers found him and took him to a field hospital where he remained for seven weeks. Meanwhile, a dead Canadian soldier who resembled him was buried under his name, and Leacock was officially reported dead. General Sam Hughes sent his family a letter of condolence.

Leacock took "French leave" from the hospital, found his way back to his regiment, and reported for duty to his commander, whose first reaction was, "Leacock, you're dead, and I can't take any spooks in my regiment. Get away back, and be content."

Leacock convinced the officer that he was flesh and blood, but had a more difficult time with the military bureaucracy. "When you're dead in the army," he told the newspaper, "they insist that you stay dead." It took months of untangling red tape before the army officially declared him alive. In the meantime, Leacock fought at the Somme, Vimy Ridge and Passchendaele. "The Hun doesn't live that can kill me," he said, "since they already killed me once."

However, Leacock was suffering from the effects of the gas. He'd finally been sent to Speedwell. Over three years, nobody had informed the newspaper that George Leacock was still alive.

Grit Callander was another Guelph soldier who had extraordinary experiences before he returned home. After his determined efforts to get into the army, he served less than a year at the front before he fell victim to trench foot. In November 1915, Callander was put aboard the hospital ship *Anglia* for the trip across the Channel to a hospital in

England. The *Anglia* struck a German mine and sank with the loss of 134 lives. Callander was among the survivors. He recovered from his affliction and went back to the trenches. By the time he returned home at the war's end, he had been awarded the Military Medal and the Belgian *Croix de Guerre*.

With the signing of the armistice, military authorities began the monumental task of transporting Canada's soldiers home. The remains of the dead would not be repatriated, but would lie in their foreign graves. More than two hundred Guelph men were buried in cemeteries in France, Belgium and England, or had been swallowed without a trace in the maw of battle and had no graves at all: Norman Brydges, George Curzon, Horace Fell, George Ryder and so many others. They were the ghosts of bereaved homes; their once-promising futures brutally denied.

In the months following the cessation of the fighting, there would be others who stepped off the train in Guelph to joyful, tearful greetings. They would return to homes that had for so long seemed to exist only in dreams or in memories of another lifetime. They would be reunited with parents or wives more aged by worry than they would otherwise have been over the passage of time since the day of parting, with children who barely remembered their fathers, with brothers and sisters who were no longer little. And for these others, their escape from the war would prove to be an illusion, because the war followed them like a stalking phantom, waiting to snatch them into the darkness.

Doctors Ernest and Clarence Young were both back in Guelph by the end of 1918. Clarence moved to Little Current on Manitoulin Island, where he established a private practice. Ernest was sent to take charge of a military hospital in Cobourg. When the hospital closed in the spring of 1920, he became assistant superintendent of a hospital for the mentally ill in Kingston. Later that year he and his wife Florence and their two children moved to London, where Ernest had been offered his old position of assistant superintendent at the Hospital for the Insane.

Ernest had lived through the Great War, but the terrible conditions at the front, and the incredible physical, psychological and emotional strain to which he had been subjected had taken a harsh toll. It caught up with him in the summer of 1921. Ernest came down with what was described as "a lingering illness." He died in London on August 8 at age forty-three. Dr. Young's funeral was held in Guelph, and he was buried in Union (now Woodlawn) Cemetery. People in Guelph were reminded that his brother was a decorated war hero.

Nursing Sister Alice Trusdale continued tending the sick and wounded overseas until she was sent home in March 1919. She was posted as a matron in the Freeport military hospital in Kitchener. During the summer, she volunteered to do relief work in Halifax, which was still recovering from the devastating explosion of December 6, 1917. By September, she was back at Freeport.

Some of the patients at Freeport had meningitis, one of the curses of overcrowded and unhygienic army camps. It was often called "soldiers' disease" and "barracks disease," and it was contagious. Trusdale fell ill in September, and although doctors didn't seem to be in agreement on the cause, she might very likely have contracted meningitis. She was taken to Guelph General Hospital, where she died on September 12 with her mother and sister at her bedside.

Dead at age twenty-seven, Alice Trusdale was buried in Waterford's Greenwood Cemetery.

Herb Philp, whose letters in the paper had provided Guelphites with vivid eyewitness accounts of the war, arrived in Guelph in July 1919 as a decorated hero. He was no longer the robust man who had gone to war in 1914. Four years of living under extreme conditions had destroyed his health.

Philp tried to resume his career as a journalist. In November, through the Soldiers' Civil Re-establishment Program, the newspaper hired him as an editor. But Philp's ruined health soon failed him. Early in January 1920, he came down with what initially seemed to be a bad cold. Philp's ailment was finally diagnosed as a heart problem caused by wartime conditions. He died in the Guelph General Hospital on January 19, twelve days short of his thirty-first birthday. Philp was buried in Woodlawn Cemetery.

When Captain James Doughty was wounded in the Battle of the Scarpe, he lay in agony at the bottom of a shell hole for almost a day before stretcher-bearers found him and carried him to a dressing station. Doughty had been shot in the abdomen and had lost a lot of blood. It seemed miraculous that he was still alive, but the doctors didn't think he had much of a chance. Soldiers who had been "gut-shot" had a low survival rate.

The doctors at the dressing station patched Doughty up as best they could, listed him as "critical," and sent him to a military hospital. There, surgeons worked to repair the damage the bullet had done to his insides. It was the first of four operations Doughty would endure in hospitals in France and England.

Doughty spent months convalescing in an English hospital. In recognition of his courage and sacrifice, his superiors promoted him to the rank of major. Over a year after the armistice, he was put aboard a ship bound for Canada. Doughty arrived in Guelph two days before Christmas of 1919.

Before the war, Doughty had been a flour, grain and feed merchant. When he returned home, he tried to re-establish himself in that business to support his wife Edna and their three children. He made a brave effort, putting on a cheerful face for the people he met every day. But those who knew him couldn't help being aware that he suffered excruciating abdominal pain. Unable to do the work his occupation demanded, Doughty had to sell his business. In 1920 he underwent a fifth operation, in Toronto.

The federal government had developed a pension and benefits program for returned soldiers who had been incapacitated. Most of those accepted were amputees and others whose handicap was plainly visible. Men who complained of the effects of disease or poison gas, debilitating pain or of mental trauma were regarded with skepticism and often rejected. Even for successful applicants, the amount of assistance usually wasn't sufficient for a man to live on, let alone support a family.

Doughty opened a grocery store. For a while he seemed to be on the road to recovery. He participated in community activities. Then, in the winter of 1921–22, the pain returned. Doughty was admitted to Guelph General Hospital, and on January 24 had his sixth operation. The doctors said the surgery was a success, and they expected a full recovery. But while Doughty was recuperating he developed a bacterial infection in his throat. Antibiotics were still unheard-of. The doctors did everything they could for Doughty, but in his weakened condition he sank quickly. At 12:30 a.m. on January 28, 1922, Doughty died with his family at his bedside.

Doughty was buried in Woodlawn Cemetery with military honours. In its front page eulogy, the newspaper said, "In his untimely end the Royal City loses a worthy son, and the country a great Canadian, of whom it can be truly said that he gave his life in the great struggle for liberty. Major Doughty was a war casualty over three years after the Great War had ended [when] his life flickered out in the quiet midnight hour . . . his memory will live long in the minds of the citizens of Guelph."

Doughty's memory, and those of the rest of the war dead, did live on in hearts and minds — for a while. There were plaques, honour rolls, and eloquent speeches at memorial services. On August 20, 1919, thousands of Guelphites lined the streets from City Hall to Exhibition Park to watch a homecoming parade of Great War veterans. The paper said, "It was the greatest day of reunion ever held in the city."

But even before the armistice, a mythology about the war and the heroics of the Canadians had evolved in hometowns like Guelph, where people had read repeatedly that their boys had "covered themselves in glory." The myth wasn't borne out by returned soldiers, who didn't want to talk about things they had seen. There was an estrangement of sorts between civilians and veterans, that was part of an overall sense of disillusionment and creeping cynicism. To many, the sacrifice in blood had not been glorious, but a needless waste of lives. Not everybody agreed with the latter part of John McCrae's poem, that began with the line "Take up our quarrel with the foe." The quarrel had been too costly and had gone on for too long. The ceremonies and monuments seemed in some minds to be a perpetuation of the myth that masked reality.

A military parade in Guelph in 1918. Canadian soldiers returning from the Western Front were unaware that many of them carried the virus that caused the deadly Spanish influenza pandemic. (Courtesy of Guelph Museums 2009.32.1998)

CHAPTER 20
AFTERMATH

News of the armistice brought almost immediate changes to daily life in war-weary Guelph. Just in time for the 1918 Christmas retail season, merchants received word from the Power Controller's office in Toronto that they would be allowed to illuminate their store windows in the evening from six o'clock until nine. Previously such lighting had been prohibited, to conserve electricity for factories doing war work. Guelph's downtown core would once again be bright during the weeks of early darkness. The Power Controller's office expressed gratitude for the merchants' uncomplaining compliance and patience with the order.

The Guelph newspaper made the much-welcomed announcement that the Canada Food Board had rescinded the regulation limiting the amount of wheat flour householders, bakeries and restaurants could purchase. Mothers would no longer have to feed their children the hated "war bread." Restaurants, which had been limited in the quantity of bread they could serve, could place sandwiches back on their menus after a long absence. Bakers could once again offer their customers cakes, doughnuts, shortbreads and French pastries; although commodities such as sugar and some cooking oils were still subject to rationing. Items like beef and butter were still in short supply, but with the end of all rationing in sight, people were happy to make do with what was available. After all, the people of Canada were better off than the people of Germany, where cities were in the grip of starvation.

There was little sympathy for the defeated enemy in Guelph or any other Canadian community. Too many families had suffered. Four years of reports of German atrocities — real or exaggerated — had seared into people's minds the image of the villainous Hun. The spectre of the German as a foe that was treacherous to the bitter end was given further credence by Swiss newspaper reports in early December 1918 that Germany had been secretly storing agents of disease in Zurich. The German army had allegedly intended to poison wells with cholera and glanders (primarily a disease of horses and mules, but one which can also affect humans) as it retreated before the advancing Allies, but for some reason hadn't had the opportunity to carry out the plan. "Poison Germs Prepared for Entente Allies" said a headline over an article that also claimed the Germans had been manufacturing munitions in Switzerland with which to aid anarchists in Italy.

Canadian newspapers said Canadians would not want to buy goods manufactured in Germany. Prior to the war, the products of German factories had been in great demand in

Canada because they were reputed to be of superior quality to those made in Canada, Britain and the United States. "Bunk! Pure and Simple Bunk!" said the newspaper.

The idea that German products were superior was the result of a prewar propaganda campaign that was part of Germany's drive for industrial supremacy, the newspaper claimed. "This country [Canada] is making better goods right now than Germany ever produced, in every line, including chemicals and drugs."

The paper warned that even after military defeat, Germany was attempting to reinstate herself as the world's best manufacturer of everything from toys to tools. "It is said that there are fifty thousand travelling salesmen singing the song of superiority of German-made goods . . . Every Canadian that is guilty of spreading such propaganda is helping to ruin the future industrial life of this nation."

Germany proper wasn't the only target of post-war fears and anger. Long-festering xenophobia erupted in the early weeks of 1919. In the wake of the defeat of the Kaiser's hordes, the enemy was now the "unfriendly aliens" living right in the midst of the victors.

Returned soldiers found that men with foreign-sounding names and thick accents were doing their old factory jobs. These were the "Austrians," the non-British immigrants who hadn't been through the hell of the Western Front. Lost in the surge of frustration and resentment were the facts that the Canadian military hadn't wanted these "aliens," and their labour had kept Canada's war industry running.

On the evening of Sunday, February 9, 1919, a capacity crowd packed the Guelph Opera House in response to a call by the Great War Veterans' Association (GWVA). Filling the seats in what the reporter called "the most wonderful meeting held in Guelph since the war started" were representatives of Guelph's merchants and manufacturers, members of city council, private citizens and hundreds of returned soldiers. The single topic of discussion was "the alien question."

After the singing of "O Canada," Mayor James E. Carter thanked the veterans for the honour they had bestowed on him in asking him to preside over the meeting, and assured them they had the support of city hall. Then he turned the podium over to Captain Archdeacon A.C. Macintosh, president of the Guelph branch of the GWVA. What Macintosh had to say went straight to the hearts of "men who had heard the call of duty in this place."

Macintosh told the audience that while Canadian soldiers were fighting and dying, the aliens in Guelph and Canada "without sacrifice" made more money than they ever could have earned in their home countries. "They are not British subjects, and do not intend to be," he said. "Their sole ambition was to save their money, made here, and return to their homeland to enjoy it . . . They are here as transients, and for their own convenience. Now, the question is, for whom is this country, the men who fought for it, or these aliens?"

A voice from the audience called out, "The Britisher, of course."

Macintosh spoke further about aliens making "big money" while Canadians "had the privilege of dodging shot and shell for $1.10 a day," only to come home to find aliens holding down all the jobs. "What we do want, in plain speech and without hedging, is a white Canada. We want the alien fired from his present position as long as there is a returned soldier in Canada who is able to work."

The next speaker was William E. Turley, provincial secretary of the GWVA. He hammered away at the same theme, that soldiers had been fighting the Hun menace for four years, and now faced a menace at home. "Our boys are walking around the streets looking for work while the aliens are drawing down big envelopes. These soldiers shouldn't be looking for a job; the job should be looking for them."

Turley warned of Canada being overrun by immigrants who "came to this country to get all they could . . . When we went away we saw big, strapping Austrians and Turks driving the pick and shovel. We return and find them driving an automobile . . . These aliens have proved that they can never become Canadian citizens. They can never become imbued with the ideals so dear to Canadians."

Turley called for the deportation of all aliens as soon as transportation could be arranged. He wanted a fifty-year ban on "enemy immigration." When he asked if returned soldiers should walk the streets while aliens held down good jobs, cries of "No! No!" rose from the audience. "It is time we made this a white man's country," Turley said.

Guelph Alderman T.J. Hannigan, who was also honorary vice-president of the Guelph branch of the GWVA, was the final speaker. He said the war wouldn't be over until every man who fought was in a better position than he was when he went away. He denounced the aliens who "got wealthy" while soldiers' pay remained $1.10 a day for the entire war, and insinuated that they refused to become Canadian citizens. He asked, "Are you going to keep such people here?"

A man in the audience shouted, "No, chloroform them!"

"All those who are not with us are against us," Hannigan declared, "and the neutrals are no better than the alien enemies."

At the meeting's conclusion, the GWVA submitted a resolution demanding (in short) that all manufacturers and employers of labour in Guelph discharge all unfriendly aliens from their employ and take on returned soldiers, "as it cannot be expected that these returning soldiers will work in harmony, side by side, with these aliens. Too much attention cannot be paid to this question in order that riots be prevented."

The resolution was passed unanimously, and it reflected ugly feelings that were being vented across the country. However, while some immigrants in Guelph might have been obliged to give up their jobs to returned soldiers, there was no mass-firing. Moreover, the newspaper reported that the question of the deportation of enemy aliens was a matter of "gradual development" that would have to be addressed by the federal government. Guelph city council did not have the issue on its agenda.

A month later, the conscription issue made headlines again, in the local paper and the Toronto *Globe*. On Saturday, March 8, a squad of Dominion Police from London commanded by an Inspector Lane arrived in Guelph. Their presence in town was kept secret. They had orders to go to the nearby community of New Germany (now Maryhill) to arrest several young men for conscription evasion, a charge as serious as that of actual military desertion. When they set out before dawn on Sunday, one of their objectives was the farm of Joseph Berberich, whose sons Anthony and George were on the wanted list.

Joseph Berberich was in bed when the police pounded on the door and demanded entry. Mrs. Berberich opened the door and showed the officers a newspaper that said the war was over. She tried to close the door, but two officers named Gaggin and Forsythe forced their way in. Mrs. Berberich grabbed a chamber pot and threw it at Gaggin, striking him on the head and spilling its contents over him. Then she began to scream.

The racket alerted her sons, who were upstairs. With Gaggin leading, the two constables started up the stairs but were confronted by one of the brothers brandishing a rifle. There was a shot, and Gaggin fell backwards, knocking over Forsythe as he tumbled down the stairs.

Anthony and George escaped through a second floor window and fled through deep snow for the cover of nearby woods. Armed with the rifle and a shotgun, they engaged in a running gunfight with pursuing officers who opened fire with revolvers. Nobody was hit, but the fugitives' gunfire kept the police at bay long enough for them to disappear into the bush.

It would have been easy to track the brothers in the snow, but Inspector Lane decided against sending his men after armed fugitives in wooded country. His first concern now was to get Constable Gaggin to the hospital in Guelph. The local newspaper reported that Gaggin had a serious head wound, but it didn't prove to be fatal.

The Berberich brothers didn't remain at large for long. The next day their father took the police to their hiding place, and convinced them to surrender. The police also arrested several other "deserters" from New Germany and the neighbouring communities of St. Agatha and Jordansberg. The prisoners were all locked in the Guelph jail. Joseph Berberich was charged with harbouring his sons, "knowing them to be defaulters."

The court hearings were held in the last week of March. Joseph Berberich was fined $100. George, who had probably shot Gaggin, was epileptic, and had his case remanded until doctors could determine his mental condition.

The magistrate told Anthony that if it weren't for a recent amendment to the law, he'd be sentenced to two years in the Kingston Penitentiary. Instead, he had the option of paying a fine of $500 plus court costs. The Guelph paper noted that Anthony was almost deaf, and if he had reported for military duty in the first place, he wouldn't have been accepted.

While discontented veterans fumed over job-stealing aliens, and the government rounded up conscription evaders, an invisible enemy invaded Canada. It reached Canadian shores with the very men who believed they had been defending their country and loved ones on the Western Front. It travelled with them on the trains that took them to their homes in communities large and small: Montreal, Toronto, Winnipeg and Vancouver; Kelowna, Medicine Hat, Moose Jaw, Kitchener and Guelph.

The influenza pandemic probably originated in China and spread westward like a deadly Biblical plague, killing millions. It reached Western Europe in 1918 and wreaked havoc on armies and civilian populations. Governments of the belligerent nations initially censored news of massive outbreaks of illness, fearful of releasing information that might be useful to the enemy. British army doctors called the mysterious killer Flanders Grippe. To their German counterparts it was *Blitz Katarrh* — Lightning Cold. When newspapers in neutral Spain reported on the horrific epidemic in their country, the English-speaking world labelled it the Spanish flu.

Medical science of the time was familiar with the symptoms of influenza, but knew very little about the virus that causes it. Doctors were helpless before the onslaught of a strain that was twenty-five times more lethal than any others the world had previously known. It killed some victims within a matter of hours, while others lingered for days. A fortunate few inexplicably recovered. Although the flu carried off children and the elderly, people in their twenties and thirties had the highest fatality rate.

Many Canadian soldiers who were officially reported to have "died of disease" on the Western Front were in all likelihood victims of the Spanish flu. Widespread illness in the ranks might have contributed significantly to the collapse and ultimate defeat of the German army. But the virus was nobody's ally and recognized no armistice. It hid itself in seemingly healthy young men as they boarded ships for home, unaware that they were carriers.

The epidemic couldn't have struck at a worse time. The war had stripped the country of doctors and nurses, and those still in Canada spent much of their time in military hospitals. A thin and unprepared line of defence stood between the population and a foe that struck suddenly and on all fronts.

Guelphites first became aware that the contagion had struck their town early in October 1918 when the paper reported a few "mostly light" cases. Readers were advised that the disease was of slight duration — no more than four days — but, "If you have a 'Diplococcus' [stinging in the nose] it's time to call the doctor."

Days later, several students at the OAC fell ill. Parts of the campus were placed under quarantine, and no students were permitted to leave the college boundaries. Dr. Henry O. Howitt, the local official for the Provincial Ministry of Health, advised that anyone with even the slightest sign of a cold refrain from visiting hospital patients. He suggested that several upcoming conventions in Guelph be cancelled, adding that he had the legal power to have them postponed indefinitely, should that be necessary.

On October 8 the paper reported that the flu had spread all over Ontario. Lieutenant Colonel J.W.S. McCullough, the Provincial Officer of Health, announced in the press, "It is the patriotic duty of every citizen to avoid influenza and keep in good health." He advised that people stay warm and dry, avoid crowds, eat plain food, abstain from alcohol and kissing and not spit in public places.

Three days later a pharmaceutical company placed a large ad in the Guelph paper under the heading "Spanish Influenza." It listed a wide selection of preventatives and remedies: kresols, peroxide, hycol, formaldehyde, eucalyptus oils, cod liver oil, aspirin tablets and a variety of cough syrups.

On October 15, the Board of Health prohibited all public gatherings in Guelph. The order shut down dance halls, theatres, billiard rooms, bowling alleys, concerts, Sunday schools and the public library. Churches were initially exempted, but soon pastors were obliged to suspend Sunday services. Schools remained open, but under the supervision of nurses. Health authorities thought it better to keep children at school under the watchful eyes of the nurses, than have them running around in the streets. An "S.O.S." call from the Board of Health appeared in the Guelph paper and other newspapers across Ontario requesting volunteers to help with the emergency. "Young women of education are urged to avail themselves of this unique opportunity to be of real service to the community."

By October 19, hundreds of Guelphites were sick, but only two deaths had been reported. Then the invisible enemy hit the city hard — as it had been doing to communities across the country. On October 22, the paper reported that at least seven residents had died in the previous twenty-four hours. One of them, Jacob Griffenham, had been put in a taxi by his doctor to be taken to the hospital. He got out of the cab at the entrance of Guelph General, and dropped dead.

The epidemic now had a hold on the city. Frightened people checked the papers for news of flu victims just as they did for war casualties. Patients who couldn't be admitted to the overcrowded hospitals lay in their sick beds at home, depending for care on family members, neighbours and doctors who were worn to exhaustion going from one stricken home to another.

Weeks passed and the death toll rose. The paper said the flu was "worse than Hun bullets," and "[The] Worst Plague Since the Black Death Swept Over the World." Because of an emergency measure that required the dead to be buried within twenty-four hours, cemetery workers required assistance from the Public Works Department in digging graves. So many nurses in Guelph General and St. Joseph's hospitals fell ill, that they had to be replaced by the nurses on school duty. By the end of October, Guelph's schools were closed.

While medical science was stymied in its efforts to find effective means to prevent and cure the disease, wild rumours spread among the lay population. Some people were certain German spies had brought the disease to North America in vials. The Guelph newspaper published a report from the United States that claimed people were vulnerable to the infection because wartime shortages had resulted in an unhealthy lack of sugar in their diet. Some people looked to their Bibles and said God was punishing the human race for the Great War. "After war comes plague!" they admonished.

Turning to ages-old defences against disease, desperate families fumigated their homes with sulphur and tobacco smoke (chain-smoking was encouraged), and scrubbed floors, walls and every stick of furniture with vinegar. They draped their windows with cheesecloth soaked in formaldehyde. Mothers applied onion, mustard and goose-grease poultices to children who so much as sniffled. Some people baked their mail in the oven in case the letters had flu germs on them.

Every remedy imaginable was brought into the fight, from coffee mixed with mustard, to quinine dissolved in whisky. While Temperance advocates swore that the demon rum was useless in combating the epidemic, in addition to being demoralizing, bottles of "medicinal" liquors flew off pharmacy shelves. One report claimed that carrying a spoonful of gin in your mouth was protection against the flu. However, it was a good idea to keep a flask in your pocket in case you accidentally swallowed the gin.

People laced their food with cinnamon and garlic, and purged themselves with laxatives. Pharmacies sold out of camphor, a pungent-smelling substance used in the manu-facture of mothballs, because people thought a little bag of the stuff worn around the neck would ward off flu germs. The newspaper offered a five-cent coupon for a preventative called Dr. Chase's Menthol Bag, which was to be worn on the chest between outer clothing and underwear.

The paper repeatedly attempted to quell panic by telling residents that local doctors and medical authorities had the epidemic under control. "There is no city in the Province that is so well off as Guelph today," one doctor said, " and it will keep the best record if instructions are obeyed to the letter . . . don't get excited: your state of mind will have much to do with your condition."

The contagion seemed to have peaked by late November. The number of reported cases suddenly dropped. Schools were reopened. Relief that the epidemic was over went hand-in-hand with joy that the war had been won.

But the respite in Guelph was typical of the Spanish flu's cruelly deceptive course. Just when the psychologically and emotionally drained citizenry thought the worst was behind them, the devil swept back with a vengeance. In the first week of December, a new rash of cases hit Guelph. Schools were closed again. Hospitals were "taxed to capacity," and grave diggers were kept busy. The siege continued until mid-January, 1919, when the number of reported deaths began to decline. The Board of Health lifted the ban on public gatherings. While in other regions of Canada the epidemic would continue to rage into spring, it had finally run its course in Guelph.

The death toll for the Spanish flu in Canada was estimated as high as sixty thousand people, meaning that in a matter of months it had killed almost as many Canadians as the Great War had done over four years. In an open letter to the people of Guelph, published in the newspaper, Dr. Howitt said that while for various reasons it was impossible to state exactly how many people in any given region had come down with the flu and how many deaths it had definitely caused, local doctors agreed that the epidemic had taken thirty-one lives in the city of Guelph, and fourteen more in neighbouring rural townships. He credited the good organization of local health officials and the splendid co-operation of the public for keeping Guelph's fatalities relatively low.

Guelph emerged from the crucibles of war and epidemic changed from the place it had been in that distant July of 1914. Like every other Canadian community it bore invisible scars. Much of the social naïveté and innocence of the

Victorian and Edwardian eras had been swept away. More than two hundred citizens that had walked its streets were gone forever.

The post-war labour strife that seethed throughout Canada and erupted in violence in Winnipeg hardly touched Guelph. The strong labour union movement suffered a setback during the war, largely because of public anger at socialist pacifism, but also because many union leaders had enlisted. There had been only a few short-lived wartime strikes. However, incidents like the returned soldiers' public manhandling of the socialist speakers reflected poorly on the city, and people wanted to put such troubles behind them.

Guelph's unions denounced radical socialism, and the city promoted itself as friendly to industrial development. Several of Guelph's older industries were bought by larger companies, and new firms were established. In spite of falling to defeat in lop-sided early post-war elections, Guelph's socialists continued their fight for improved workplace conditions and working-class living standards. The Communist Party of Canada was born at a clandestine meeting in a barn outside Guelph on May 28, 1921.

By 1924, Guelph's population had grown to twenty thousand. According to city boosters, it had the second-lowest unemployment rate in Canada. Moreover, its foreign population had been "well-absorbed." The optimistic report on high employment may have been misleading, because layoffs accompanied the rise and fall of industrial fortunes. This was somewhat offset by families having more than one member in the workforce.

By the mid-1920s, Guelph was a thriving industrial town, with all the attendant benefits and problems. The war, while not fading from memories, was being replaced by new concerns. There was a need for a permanent reminder. In 1927, the centennial of the city's founding, the Guelph Cenotaph was erected; one of thousands across Canada. The monuments remain tangible connections to the war and those who were lost. But as the Greek word *cenotaph* says, they are empty tombs. The war's real legacy lay with those who had survived the trenches, and those who had endured at home. They would carry it through two tumultuous decades, and into yet another war.

ACKNOWLEDGEMENTS

I wish to express my gratitude to all those who helped make this book possible: the many people in Guelph and Wellington County who shared their family histories when I was doing my Guelph Cenotaph project for the *Mercury*; Phil Andrews, former managing editor of the *Mercury*, for giving my project the green light and for his subsequent encouragement; Eric Huber, for sharing numerous historical documents; Guelph historian Bonnie Durtnall, creator of the excellent website www.labouringallourlives.ca; James Lorimer for entrusting me with this book, and all of the people on the editorial staff at James Lorimer Publishers for their help and patience. My thanks to Library and Archives Canada for its invaluable website "Soldiers of the First World War." Thanks also to Guelph Museums, Kitchener Public Library, Waterford Heritage & Agricultural Museum, Waterloo Historical Society and Wellington County Museum and Archives for the use of their photographs. I am very grateful to the Ontario Arts Council for a Writers' Reserve grant.

Finally, as always, I must thank the staff of the Guelph Public Library for their help when I was scouring the microfilm archives of the *Mercury* and other sources of local and national history for the First World War period. My daily presence in the library was noted by at least one patron, because she stopped by the microfilm reader where I was working and asked me, "Do you live here?"

BIBLIOGRAPHY

Black, Dan and John Boileau, *Old Enough to Fight: Canada's Boy Soldiers of the First World War*, James Lorimer & Company Ltd., Publishers, Toronto, 2013

Bowker, Alan, *A Time Such as There Never Was Before*, Dundurn Press, Toronto, 2014

Chadwick, W.R., *The Battle for Berlin, Ontario*, Wilfrid Laurier University Press, Waterloo, 1992

Dancocks, Daniel G., *Spearhead to Victory: Canada and the Great War*, Hurtig Publishers, Edmonton, 1987

Gwyn, Sandra, *Tapestry of War*, Harper Collins, Toronto, 1992

Johnson, Leo A., *The History of Guelph: 1827–1927*, Guelph Historical Society, Guelph, 1977

Matheson, Dawn and Rosemary Anderson (Eds), *Guelph: Perspectives on a Century of Change, 1900–2000*, Guelph Historical Society, Guelph, 2000

McKegney, Patricia P., *The Kaiser's Bust*, Bamberg Heritage Series, Bamberg Press, Wellesley, 1991

Ross, Alexander and Terry Crowley, *The College on the Hill: A New History of the Ontario Agricultural College*, Dundurn Press, Toronto, 1999

Rutherdale, Robert, *Hometown Horizons: Local Responses to Canada's Great War*, UBC Press, Vancouver, 2004

Wilson, Barbara M. (ed.), *Ontario and the First World War, 1914–1918*, The Champlain Society for the Government of Ontario, University of Toronto Press, Toronto, 1977

Woolley, Max, *Callanders of Guelph*, Library of Wellington County Branch OGS, undated

The Guelph *Mercury*

The Toronto *Globe*

The *OAC Review*

www.espritdecorps.ca/rehabilitation-and-retraining

www.cbc.ca/history/
EPISCONTENTSE1EP12CH2PA5LE.html

www.wartimecanada.ca/essay/learning/education-during-first-world-war

www.rmslusitania.info/related-ships/hesperian

www.labouringallourlives.ca

INDEX

Allied forces, 31–32, 37–38, 40, 44, 49, 89, 91–92, 108, 111, 122, 160, 164, 175, 207, 210, 214–15, 233, 235–36, 238–40, 244, 260

armistice, 165, 232, 239–40, 244, 249, 252, 255–56, 259, 267

Armoury, 9, 26, 27, 28, 29, 55–56, 122, 201–202, 213

army
    Austro–Hungarian, 20
    British, 20–21, 29, 43, 71, 137
    Canadian, 9, 24–25, 27, 33, 35, 70, 78, 84, 112, 125, 199
    German, 40, 46, 236, 239, 260, 267
    recruitment, *see* recruiting
    Russian, 20, 233

Army Chaplain Service, 74, 108
    volunteers, 59, 106, 108, 248

Army Medical Corps, 28, 87, 89, 110, 135–36, 138–42, 170, 177, 221

Austrians, 19–20, 154, 263
    in Guelph, 20, 26–27, 195, 199–201, 203, 261

awards, 91, 92, 140, 243, 245, 252

Baxter, William, 21, 29, 35

Belgium, 19, 25, 37–38, 49–50, 59, 69, 88, 91, 109, 155, 160, 174, 177, 185–86, 227, 252

Berlin, Ontario, 15, 152–63, 195

Boer War, 10, 24, 31, 48, 52, 84, 105, 113, 135, 148

Borden, Robert, 24, 28, 52, 117–19, 122, 154, 177, 197, 219

Bourque, Henri, 123–25, 127–30, 133

Boy Scouts, 88–89, 197–98, 212

Britain, 9, 10, 31–32, 40, 238
    allegiance to, 17, 20, 24–25, 29, 37, 57–58, 61–63, 97–99, 108, 120, 146, 154, 157, 195, 198–201, 210, 220, 239

Guelph population, 17, 28–29, 57, 84, 199, 210, 252, 262

cadets, 10–11, 96, 197–99, 212

Callander, Wilfrid Laurier, "Grit," 23–24, 28, 30, 35, 39, 48, 61, 251–52

Canadian Patriotic Fund, 52, 89, 91, 177, 186–91

Carter, Samuel, 12, 14, 29, 58, 184

Cenotaph, 7, 273

children, war involvement, 86–93, 197–98, 212

churches, 15, 29, 59, 92, 107–11, 119, 122, 130–32, 154, 182, 185, 212, 248, 268

citizenship
    diverse, 14, 18, 126, 210, 263
    duties, 98, 105, 177, 190, 219, 268
    war involvement, 10, 187, 219, 223, 271

comfort parcels, 179–83

conscription, 116–20, 122–24, 126–27, 132–33, 137, 177, 219–31, 233–34, 244, 264–66

Conscription Act, 118, 121–22, 222, 244

Courcelette, Battle of, 214–15

Creelman, George C., 95, 100, 104, 105

Cunningham, Lorne, 119, 223–27, 230

Daily Herald, 16, 97

deaths
    influenza, 266–69, 271
    mistaken, 49, 69–70, 79–80, 250–51
    soldier, 35, 41–43, 48, 53, 65–81, 83, 86, 110, 112, 114, 120, 139, 141–43, 161, 164–65, 179, 234–35, 237–41, 249, 252, 254

discrimination
    ethnic, 17–18, 26, 90, 154–57,
        177, 192, 199–200, 202, 261
    soldiers' dependents, 205-206
Doughty, James, 11, 234–35, 254–56
England, *see* Britain
enlisting, 12, 22–23, 25, 28, 30,
        34–35, 45, 54–61, 68, 71,
        80–81, 84–86, 88, 100, 105,
        112, 115, 118, 121–22, 135–36,
        140, 143, 145, 153, 157,
        168–72, 213, 217–20, 244
epidemics
    measles, 89–90
    influenza, 266–71
equipment, 25
    faulty, 27, 44, 61, 147, 180–82
Exhibition Park, 14, 19, 29, 33, 34,
        92, 256
Expeditionary Force, Canadian,
        11, 36–37, 40, 42, 44, 49, 57,
        66–69, 78, 83, 84, 108, 112,
        117, 153, 163, 164, 168, 177,
        186, 188, 214, 219, 237, 243
Farley, Albert, 223–24, 226–28
Flanders Fields
    battle of, 35, 86, 250, 266
    poem, 7, 96
food, 33, 149–51, 180, 259–60
    rationing, 31–32, 38, 175–76,
        184, 260
fundraising, 28–30, 87–89, 174,
        183–91
    fraudulent, 185–86
Galt, John, 15, 162
George, King, 15, 17, 79, 120, 159,
        186
    "God Save the King," 17, 29,
        34, 91, 158, 187, 229, 230,
        231
Germans, 153–58
    in Guelph, 26, 27, 90, 97–98, 122,
        161–62, 193–95, 197–98,
        260
    prisoners, 47, 161
    spies, 25–26, 47, 155, 158, 161,
        193–203, 269

wrongfulness, 29, 37–38, 40, 43,
        48, 50, 56, 58, 60, 87, 90,
        108, 157–60, 175, 193–203,
        214, 260
    see also Berlin, Ontario
Globe, Toronto, 27, 97, 196, 198, 264
Governor General, 186
    Cup, 11
    visit, 120, 212
"Grit" Callandar, *see* Callander,
        Wilfrid Laurier "Grit"
Guthrie, Hugh, 58, 119, 121, 123
Hayes, Lewis, 42, 66, 125, 222
heatless days, 208–209
Hughes, Sam, 11, 19, 25, 28, 44, 52,
        181, 202, 251
immigrants, 17–18, 20, 28, 57, 70,
        83, 90, 153–55, 172, 177, 186,
        195–200, 202–203, 261–64, 272
Imperial Order of the Daughters of
        the Empire (IODE) *see* IODE
IODE, 29, 86, 120, 174, 188
Ireland, Richard A., 14, 136–39
Kitchener, Ontario, *see* Berlin,
        Ontario
Langemarck, Battle of, 40, 42, 45–47,
        49, 250–51
Laurier, Wilfrid, 97, 119
letters
    editorial, 43, 57, 97, 99–100,
        104–05, 164, 167–69, 196,
        205, 233, 244, 248
    soldiers', 39, 43–50, 61, 64, 68,
        71-78, 85–86, 112–14,
        141–42, 181–82, 219, 234–35
Lusitania, 43, 66, 238
Macaulay, A.C., 124–30, 133
Macdonell Street, 13, 213, 223
manliness, 10, 56, 61, 143, 170–72,
        217, 221
McCrae, John, 7, 24, 256–57
medical
    equipment, 89, 247
    staff shortage, 190, 135–38, 143,
        267
Mennonites, 122, 126, 153–54, 195
Mercury, Guelph, 7, 15–16, 18–19,

25–26, 30, 34, 36, 38, 47,
59, 61–63, 66, 68–69, 89, 92,
97–98, 104–105, 120, 139–40,
146, 167–68, 179, 182–83,
199–201, 203, 214, 234,
237–38, 245, 248, 250, 259,
264, 267–68, 270
militarism, 9, 10, 26, 28, 86, 103–105,
118, 148, 212–14, 223–25
military police, 123
    raids, 8, 116, 121, 124–33
Military Service Act see Conscription Act
militias
    community, 9–11, 184, 25–26,
        138, 153, 158–59, 174, 196
    Guelph, 9–10, 26, 27–28, 96,
        102–105, 183–84, 187, 201
    at war, 11, 25, 27–29, 37–38,
        49–51, 183
newspapers, 117, 121, 128, 137,
    182–83, 196–97, 219–20,
    233–34
    discrimination, 17, 122, 203,
        260–61
    international, 20, 43, 260, 266,
        268
    support for war, 28, 30–31, 33, 38,
        40–41, 43–44, 59, 62–63,
        69–70, 80–81, 87, 91, 120,
        122, 128, 132, 146–47, 155,
        159, 167–70, 174, 190, 215,
        236, 245
Novitiate, St. Stanislaus, 116, 121–33
nurses, 28, 90, 135–37, 140–43, 170,
    177, 242, 247, 253, 267–69
Ontario Agricultural College, 14, 31,
    61, 95–97, 99–105, 184, 240,
    244–45, 267
Opera House, 16, 58–59, 94,
    101–104, 188–89, 213, 221–22,
    230, 251, 261–62
pacifism, 95–100, 171, 176
Passchendaele, 138, 165, 233, 251
Patriotic Fund, 52, 89, 91, 177,
    186–91
patriotism, 22, 24, 29, 33, 34, 56,
    58, 60–63, 66, 86, 88–89,

91, 96–98, 115, 122, 145–51,
    154–57, 169–72, 174–75, 177,
    185–87, 212, 214, 221, 225,
    231, 260–61, 268
Pearson, Lester B., 110–11
Philp, Herbert, 11, 39, 49–51, 53,
    219–20, 234, 254
prisoners of war, 43, 47, 67, 78–79,
    215, 236, 241
propaganda, 38, 78, 91, 144, 147,
    157, 214–16, 261
    see also patriotism
Railway, Grand Trunk, 19, 26, 139,
    208–209
rallies, 34, 58–59, 91, 109, 115, 221
Randall, Frederick, 16, 26, 27, 192,
    199–202, 222
recruiting, 23, 28, 30, 54–59, 88, 109,
    111, 115, 117, 120, 122, 140,
    147, 153, 157–58, 169–71, 212,
    216–21
Red Cross Society, 29, 30, 76, 79,
    163–64, 174, 185, 211
religious
    conflict, 16, 96, 118, 121–22,
        128–33
    support for war, 59–61, 107–112,
        115, 119, 132, 154
Reformatory, Ontario, 14, 29, 188,
    246–47
Respa, Charles, 193–95, 203
returned soldiers, 51, 53, 79, 92,
    165, 172, 174, 212, 221, 234,
    243–52, 261–64
Riverside Park, 13, 211
Ross rifle, 44, 61
Royal Flying Corps, 11, 33, 110–11
Royal Navy, 20, 25, 28, 32, 58, 147
Russia, 19–20, 37, 59, 160, 233, 234,
    244
Salvation Army, 53, 178, 187, 240
schools, 10, 14, 17, 24, 86–88, 90,
    99–105, 154–55, 161, 174–75,
    268–71
Secord, Laura, 18
shortages, 18, 87, 136–37, 143, 150–51,
    163, 175, 184, 204–11, 269

"slackers," 56, 100, 109, 117, 122,
    158, 167–70, 172, 211, 219
socialists, 176, 223–31
Somme, Battle of, 138, 214, 233, 251
South Wellington Conservative
    Association, 97–98
Spanish influenza, 258, 266–71
St. George's Square, 13, 16, 54, 230
St. Patrick's Ward *see* Ward, the
training, military, 10, 25, 28, 37,
    61–62, 96–97, 100, 108, 111,
    145
Trusdale, Alice, 134, 136, 142–43,
    253–54
uniforms, 34, 56, 92, 105, 109, 117,
    132, 148, 211
    cadet 10–11
    manufacturing 25, 82, 90, 181–82,
    249
unions, 16–17, 272
United States, 14, 26, 32, 109,
    155, 186, 193–94, 196, 201,
    207–208, 220, 233, 261, 269
Valcartier, 28, 30, 34, 81, 157
Veterans' Association, 34, 68, 187,
    246, 249, 261
Vimy Ridge, 69, 138, 164, 250–51
volunteering, 11, 28–29, 30, 33–34,
    55, 57, 78, 83, 100, 105, 108,
    112, 117, 120, 137, 139–40,
    145, 147, 153, 157–58, 213,
    216, 218, 221, 247
war
    of 1812, 18
    Boer *see* Boer War
    Canadian participation, 21–22,
    24, 25–26, 28, 31–33, 36,
    40, 44–46, 87–88, 98, 105,
    135–36, 139–43, 146–47, 153,
    167–72, 215, 236–38, 247
    costs of, 31, 52–53, 65–81, 83,
    86, 110, 112, 114, 120, 139,
    141–43, 150–51, 185, 216,
    234, 237–41, 243–45
    films, 214–15
    international participation, 19–20,
    25, 37–38, 40, 44, 46, 58–59,

    66, 98, 108, 111, 122, 160,
    164, 175, 207, 210, 214–15,
    233, 235–37, 260
    mock, 212–13, 215
    unprepared for, 9, 11, 18–19, 44
    weapons, 40–41, 43, 46–47,
    50–51, 58, 74, 76, 79–80, 87,
    139, 143, 148, 190, 193–95,
    202, 215, 235, 240
Ward, the, 14, 16, 18, 30, 195
War Measures Act, 38, 195, 198
Wartime Elections Act, 177
Welland Canal, 25–26
Wellington County, 10, 18, 26, 33,
    41, 153
Western Front, 11, 39–42, 57, 64, 67,
    106, 111, 115, 117, 136, 147,
    151, 155, 159, 165, 181, 215,
    219, 234–37, 240, 244, 258,
    261, 266, 267
Wilhelm (I, II), Kaiser, 23, 38, 129,
    152, 154–159, 162, 165, 191,
    195–97, 214, 234, 261
wireless radio, 27, 192
women
    employment, 17, 84, 90,
    172–174, 199
    war involvement, 29, 57–59, 84, 91,
    100, 136–37, 166–70, 172–77,
    180–82, 187, 206, 268
Woolwich Street, 29, 213
Wyndham Street, 13, 29, 55, 177,
    213, 230, 239, 240
Young, Ernest, 136, 139, 252–53
Ypres, second battle, 36, 40, 42, 43,
    44, 45–47, 49, 52, 57, 66, 78,
    245
Zavitz, Charles A., 95–100, 105